A car and two lads

Ted Prangnell

New Generation Publishing

Credits and Acknowledgements

Barry Risbridger
> Who designed and built the frame for the hood, re-sprayed the car "Esso" Red, and cut vent holes in the side of the engine compartment.

Linda and Brian Mock
> Who carried out the initial edit.

Barbara Benedict
> Who took on the daunting task of bringing order out of my chaos, and who gave unlimited support and encouragement to the author. One who experienced the thrill of travelling as passenger in Droopy Drawers, and lived to tell the tale.

Mike Jarrett.
> Passenger and co-driver.

Ted, as he looked in the early 1950s

CONTENTS

FOREWORD

"Getting to know the Continent in an Austin-Seven"

Continental travel was not a venture to be taken lightly in the 1950's especially in a car that had just been purchased, was old, second or even third or even fourth hand (who knows?), and one that was in a somewhat imperfect condition. That, however, was what I did and am still alive to tell the tale. My companion, Mike, suffered with me and I say 'suffered' without a hint of exaggeration or facetiousness. Any sane person would have asked why we did not turn back at the first sign of trouble, but we were young and headstrong and a sense of adventure was in the air, we did not want anything to come between the promise of new experiences, of seeing 'glamorous' countries for ourselves, etc.

First, we had to get the car and ourselves across the Channel. This we did by using a ferry service that operated between Dover and Ostend. These services were much more rudimentary compared with how they are today. For a start the ships were smaller, the services were far less frequent, and were often delayed by bad weather. The facilities on board were basic and they were not fitted with stabilisers to reduce the effect of a choppy sea.

Once on the Continent itself we found that the state of the roads was generally very bad, apart from the few Autobahns in Germany. One of which in Belgium, ran from Ostend to Brussels, which had been built during the Second World War to facilitate speedy German troop movements to and from the coast. It was not, as we found out, very pleasant to drive on as it had only two lanes and the surface was constructed with large slabs of concrete, the gaps between them were in-filled with tar. As a consequence the car's wheels thumped over every joint –

verdump, verdump, verdump. Car suspension was not very good on the best of vehicles in those days and my car was particularly badly off in that respect. We found that the minor roads were dreadful, often comprised of and surfaced with rough fieldstones, or horrendously large cobbles. One could imagine that some roads had been left as they were by the Romans and had not been repaired since! English roads were by comparison generally better. Traffic road signs were much less informative than in Britain, but the continental signs dramatically improved later, after a consensus was arrived at by members of the EEC. Most of these signs were consequently adopted by Britain too and in many other places in the world today.

In the 1950s Europe was not one large family as it is today. Each country was distinct and quite separate, and had its own rules for foreign travel. There was one thing, however, they were in agreement about and that was the 'import' and 'export' of cars. Travelers taking their own car round the Continent and across borders had to import and export it in and out of every country they passed through. This entailed a lot of tedious paperwork. Also there was the currency issue. At every border one had to change money into French Francs, Belgium Francs, Dutch Guilders, and German Marks.

The MOT was unheard of in the UK and it was the same in all Continental countries. There was no compulsory use of seatbelts (they may not have been fitted) and there was nothing to help the driver in the way of efficient windscreen wipers or de-misters and heating was absent from the majority of cars. Synchromesh gearboxes were the latest things to be fitted on the more popular new cars, but more often than not they were only fitted to smooth out the two higher ratio gears. It was normal to double-de-clutch for the bottom gear. One used hand signals to indicate when turning left or right at junctions, and to show that you were slowing down or stopping, as there were no braking-lights to warn following drivers. Only newer cars had indicators, which were known as 'winkers' or 'flashers'. These Indicators were little, illuminated semaphore arms that popped out from either side of the car so that the driver did not have to wind down a window and stick his hand out to signal, which was unpleasant especially in the pouring rain or in the cold of winter, and to make things worse they were notoriously unreliable. Even when taking a Driving-Test in a car fitted with trafficators, the student had to demonstrate to the examiner that he (or she) knew all the hand signals even though the car you were driving might have been fitted with the more modern devices. And, of course in the heat of summer there was not the luxury of air-conditioning. As Droopy was not parked in a garage, her cooling system had to be drained off at the slightest hint of a frost. And with a leaky system like hers, and the high price of antifreeze, I could not afford to leave her with the coolant in the system over night, it might all leak out or freeze up

Today (2015) we take for granted all the 'mod cons' that come with the modern car. Now, by comparison we are really spoiled, and this story may leave one with raised eyebrows but it happens to be true then. Mike and I set off on our adventure full of anticipation without the slightest idea of what the trip would have in store for us; but we found out soon enough, and more so as we went along.

Aspects of Austin-7s

Mike obligingly tops up Droopy's radiator. Perhaps we should have been more aware, and taken notice of, such warning signs as Droopy's very apparent thirst.

Droopy started off its life as a 1928 Austin-7 van, Such as this one. This could have been it, who knows?

[Courtesy of Ed Thompson Otford Historical Society]

George's 'Red-Devil'

Jack's 'Limmo'

Why 'DROOPY-DRAWERS'?

Droopy-Drawers is a strange name to give to a car, but like a lot of cars loved by their owners I bestowed this name on mine out of affection. She may have given the appearance of a sprightly little racer, and a little racer she certainly did look, but her top speed was, at best, 65 mph (going down hill). That was just about all I could squeeze out of her. When climbing hills her pace was somewhat slower and she often laboured to say the least. Somehow I do not think her performance would have suited the likes of James Bond.

My father's car, in which I passed my test in 1957, had been a 1938 Morris 8 (Series E), four-cylinder side valve engine. It was a well-loved domestic vehicle, a faithful friend that stayed in the family until 1960, was named 'Esmeralda' a name that was suggested by her number plate, ESM22. It was not only our family who gave names to their cars. It was common practice especially as people at that time kept their car for many years and did grow attached to their vehicles. I like to think that older cars tend to have more character.

I chose the name 'Droopy-Drawers' for my wagon, because to me, she seemed to need stronger elastic to hold herself together. Its propulsion unit was a little under par and it was not only new and stronger elastic that was needed which I found out soon after I had bought her. It was perhaps just as well that she did not go very fast as her braking capabilities were appalling. Despite that, and all her other faults, she looked terrific and was a great crowd-puller. She attracted people's interest and turned heads wherever she went. Another of her endearing features was her loud harmonious, burbling exhaust note. That was another very important aspect for an egoistic young man – as, no doubt I was at that age, Droopy was very attractive to the young ladies of the time. I hasten to add that I did not buy her for that reason. That only became apparent over time.

My first ever motor vehicle had been a 1947, 350cc 'AJS' motorbike which I purchased in 1954 for £60. This happened to be the sum total of my Post Office savings and all I could afford. I bought the bike from a motor sales business in The Old Kent Road in London. At the time I was doing my National Service in the RAF based in Somerset and I wanted some cheap transport to get me out and about and periodically to get me to my home in Kent. However, I soon discovered that motorcycling does have its drawbacks. It was often decidedly inconvenient .... having to dress up in protective clothing every time one wanted to go out on the bike for however short a journey, and then there was the danger involved in riding in bad weather. Friends, especially if they were female, were rather disinclined to ride pillion, especially as 'mummy' did not like their daughters to be put in danger on such a precarious vehicle and as, in those days, daughters were expected to do what they were told. So it was not often I could take a companion with me when I wanted to go out socialising. Most of my friends and acquaintances had cars, almost exclusively Austin 7s and those who wanted to go one better had 'Sporty Specials', although I do remember that one acquaintance had a Morgan three-wheeler (which was in itself quite a sporty machine). Most of the Austin 7 cars had been converted by their owners in their garages and some of them looked very good. They were referred to as 'specials'. I was a member of the Young Conservatives at that time *(everyone has a skeleton in their cupboard)* and I even rose to the high seat of Chairman of the Otford group. We certainly did not join the club out of any political leanings; we were just a group of healthy youngsters who had a tremendous amount of good clean fun. We did not give politics a single thought. One of the major items listed on our entertainments program was a treasure hunt round the countryside which involved cars and we also mingled with other branches of the club for evening entertainments. To get to these events one had to have transport even if one could share a car sometimes with someone else. The ownership of a car was the key to being in the group and I had to have a think about how I could solve my transport problems. I had to have a car!

Firstly I had to pass the driving test and that required the loan of my father's dear Esmeralda. The fact that when I was in the RAF I had been, amongst other things, a tractor driver had certainly helped. I only took a few driving lessons before I went for the test. I clearly remember carrying out an emergency stop during the test. The examiner warned me before hand that he was about to require me to make an emergency stop. The method was that he would strike the dashboard with his clipboard and shout, "Stop". As we drove around the town there came a moment when I sensed what he was about to do just that, his clipboard twitched a fraction, and I was ready for it. Just as he struck the dashboard with it I had already banged my foot down on the brake pedal, and the poor examiner's red face hit the windscreen quite hard. There were no seatbelts to hold him back in those days so he was thrown sharply forward without being able to protect himself. The Morris's brakes were excellent! As that moment had just illustrated. When he recovered and gathered himself and his papers together; picking some up from the floor, he turned towards me, wriggled his nose like a rabbit and said slowly and quietly, "I won't ask you to do that again, Mr. Prangnell."

I passed! At the first attempt! I was anxious he might fail me out of spite after the braking incident but fortunately for me, he did not. When I got home my father was very surprised that I had passed and I am not so sure that he was even pleased. As I had the papers for a real driving licence now all I needed was a Motor.

The Austin-7 craze

Most of my friends seemed to have got Austin-7s many of them had souped them up, or customised the bodywork

Mike's 'Little Hornet'

Dave's 'Juliana'

Malcolm's 'Yellow-peril'
(Camping in Cornwall)

They 'pulled' the girls

I just had to have one!

"Droopy Drawers"

"A bargain?"

I started to look for a car of my own whilst at the same time I advertised my AJS motorbike in a paper called the Exchange & Mart. However, the advertisement did not bring any buyer to the door nor did I receive one single enquiry. So in frustration, I eventually sold the bike back to the same company from whom I had bought it, Pride and Clarke, of Stockwell Road, for the miserly sum of £10. It did nothing for my 'pride' having to part with my motorcycle for such a pittance. It was a virtual give-away. In the meantime a colleague at work told me that he knew of an Austin 7 that was for sale near where he lived in Norwood, south London. What excited me was that he told me that it was 'special', so at the earliest opportunity I dashed off to Norwood at the weekend to have a shufti (take a look). And there it was, a special, I was hooked the moment I saw it. A better word would have been 'enchanted'. To my inexperienced eye, it looked better than most of my friends' 'specials'. It was painted in British Racing Green and it had what was described as a 'tonneau' cover. My, that looked smart. I was certainly impressed right down to my toes.

"Just wait till the lads at home hear about this", I thought. There was more! It had a remote gear lever. Genuine MG lever mechanism! Also it had a steering wheel from an MG fitted and it also had leather straps to hold the bonnet on and to crown everything, it had beautiful, sumptuous, large Marcel chromium-plated headlights. By the time my eye had finished taking everything in I must have been drooling; I had fallen in love with her, hook line and sinker. When the engine was demonstrated. I was impressed as it started up, and I heard the sweet engine note. I made a quick decision. I could hardly believe my luck. Mr. Toad could not have been more infatuated. All I saw in front of me was a perfect little beauty and it could be all mine for a mere £60. The deal was done and I became the proud owner of a sporty Austin 7. I was in Austin Seventh Heaven.

I do not suppose for a moment the car would have passed an "AA" inspection or an MOT had there been any such thing then. I was so taken in, so besotted that I was not looking for faults. On the way, driving home, I soon found them.

I have to admit that the owner, on the point of sale, had casually remarked that the brakes needed attention and that he had not quite got around to doing them. My auto engineering experience was very limited, however, I had managed to change the brake shoes on my motorcycle so I thought confidently that I should be able to accomplish that little job on an Austin 7. No, it should not present too much of a problem for me, or so I thought! The vendor must have been greatly relieved not to have had to demonstrate the overall capabilities of his car by taking me for a test drive, his relief being matched by the great and absolute delight of the purchaser, Muggins, that's me. My examination of the vehicle was carried out looking through rose-coloured spectacles. I was seduced by its appearance but should have known better, even at my youthful age, never to judge a book by its cover. All I could think of was the impression it would make on family and friends, an impression equal to that which it had on me. What magic!

I am almost six feet tall with rather long legs. Immediately I had purchased the car I realised I had to learn a special technique in order to get into the driving seat. The large diameter steering wheel did not help at all. More or less, I had to stand up in the driver's position then slide my straight left leg under the dashboard with my right leg tucked under my left knee to get into the seated driving position. It required a bit of practice, but over time it became second nature. However on this particular day, after I had got myself settled I said goodbye and was off. I drove my 'new toy' nervously and cautiously home soon finding out the truth about the brakes. They were almost non-existent. I knew how to double-de-clutch as I had to do that on our Morris-8 to get into bottom gear, so I did not find that a problem. I was also fairly used to the advance and retard timing as I had had that on the motorbike. Initially, apart from the brakes, I found it fun to drive and enjoyed the attention it seemed to attract. I was a little disappointed with the hooter which could only emit a pathetic 'Err-Er-er'' It was an electric klaxon such as was fitted on all Austin 7 cars at that time but for me it was an exceedingly pathetic sound and extremely embarrassing. It did not go with the image of the car at all or the image I would like to have portrayed. Unfortunately, nothing in this life is perfect but as I looked upon the hooter's sound as the car's only failing it did not dampen the delight in my purchase.

I arrived home and swung the car into our drive flushed with pride and brimming with pleasure at the thought of the impression I would create with my new toy. I switched off the engine and was just about to press the horn to attract the folks indoors when I remembered just in time the dreadful "Eer-er-er" noise it made. I thought for a few seconds and then had a better idea. I restarted the engine and revved it up a few times and then with careful adjustment of the advance and retard a loud backfire sound ensued. "Verroom, Bang!" "That cannot fail to wake them up and I will not have to wait long for a reaction," thought I.

It did. Our green front door opened wide and out came my elder brother with his eyebrows raised with pleasant surprise and a smile on his face. He was followed by my mother screwing up her apron, she looked surprised and a little unsure; and she probably could not decide what to think. Then finally, out came my father with a look of horror on his face. It was very apparent that he was neither impressed, nor amused, and certainly not pleased. All this rather put a damper on what I had wanted to be a triumphal homecoming.

I suppose, looking back, part of my father's concern was understandable, because; overnight we had suddenly jumped from being a two car household, to three and it was going to cause parking problems. Something I had not given any thought to, nor anticipated, so determind was I to get a car. After some debate in the family, we eventually agreed to get around this problem (to some extent) by removing a portion of a flowerbed at the front of the house (something else my father was not especially pleased about, as one can imagine) thereby making a patch large enough to fit Droopy Drawers in. She was an extraordinarily slim little vehicle, so with very precise parking I was able to tuck my little car away quite neatly. No space was required to allow for doors to open because, quite simply, she did not have any.

So the arrival of my car was not a popular addition to the family as far as my parents were concerned and in particular for my father, but the die was cast and they tolerated her in a way realising perhaps that cars were a fact of life and most young men felt the need to have one especially as we lived in a village. If one wanted to be mobile, then private transport was a useful acquisition.

I soon found out that my friends and acquaintances were very keen to be introduced to my car and to have a ride in her. What pleased me more was that the girls I knew were particularly seduced by her charm. The first time I took a girl out for a spin in the car I became aware of one of her rather dubious and hitherto un-anticipated devilish characteristics. The girl in question (it might have been Barbara Benedict ~ see credits) was wearing a light broad hemmed cotton skirt and as I got up to a certain speed the airflow over the windscreen developed a suction, which whipped up my passenger's skirt without warning. From then on she had a struggle to keep her skirt over her knees. It was surprising how I completely forgot to warn any future female passengers who were travelling in Droopy for the first time.

One girl with whom I enjoyed a platonic relationship with, was a good friend called Jill. She was a particularly jolly and attractive acquaintance who I eventually persuaded to come out for drive. However Jilly was no silly. She must have been forewarned for when I arrived at her home to collect her she came to the front door wearing slacks. In those days girls in trousers or slacks were a fairly uncommon sight, but Jill knew her onions and had taken the precaution of wearing something more appropriate for a ride in an open topped car. Jill was always great fun to have around and because of the trousers she earned the nickname of "Jillybags". She remains a life-long friend.

My car has arrived

In the sun sporting its smart Tonneau cover.

Prepared for rain. With the hood up.

17

Jillybags
and Droopy

Droopy parked in the drive at home

What a little cracker!

Our drive is filling up

"Assessing the Drawbacks"

I needed to drastically improve the stopping capability of my treasured machine. I managed to fit a completely new set of brake shoes all round. However this seemed to make little difference to improving the effectiveness of the brakes. They were cable operated and any adjustment to them was made by altering the tension in the cables with a device which gripped the cables with two claws, in between which was a screw-down clamp. This, in effect, bent the cable and in doing so altered its length (shortened it). It was a crude concept and not very effective at the best of times and it made little difference to the brakes' efficiency. The best I could achieve was a slight tendency for the off-side rear wheel to lock slightly when the brakes were applied hard; that was the only wheel that it affected. After some examination I eventually established why the brakes were so poor. The car had started off in life as a little 'sit-up-and-beg' delivery van, and a very small one at that. The entire original body had been removed and discarded, all except for the chromium plated radiator surround. A completely new body had been re-fabricated which was designed to give it a "sporty" image and was somewhat lower than the original. To achieve this sleeker, lower profile it had been necessary to carry out some rather drastic surgery on the steering column which was now set at a more "rakish" angle. This steering column was mounted on a tube that was built transversely across the car frame or chassis. The revised angle of the steering column had caused the tube to rotate anti-clockwise through about 20 degrees and unfortunately this same tube carried the handbrake levers and also the levers that worked the foot-brake pedal. These levers pulled the cables in response to the application of the foot and hand brakes, working in a similar principal as the operating mechanism of the old semaphore railway signal cables. The effect of altering the angle of this all-important tube had been to change the angle of the pivoting break cable operating levers, so that they tended to lift the cables up, instead of generating the necessary horizontal pull. In effect, the brakes had been sacrificed for appearances sake!

Eventually, I realised, the truth had to be faced. There was nothing that could be done to improve the brakes unless the braking system could be changed altogether, say to a hydraulic one (there were conversion kits available at the time), otherwise I was never going to have effective brakes of any consequence on my car. In the meantime I was forced to rely heavily on slick gear changing to slow the car down. Forward thinking, keen anticipation and very adept management of the gears by double-de-clutching, and with the help of that one wheel that locked on braking, I managed to stop the car whenever necessary. With the throaty exhaust notes that the car gave out, the whole driving experience to me, seemed pretty impressive. It was good fun really, or so it seemed in those days and I learned to live without using the one brake I had most of the time.

The lowering of the bodywork had other quite serious consequences on the mechanics of the car and indeed its thermodynamics. To suit the lowered bonnet line, the radiator also had to be lowered. Was this a simple matter? Not on your life! With the radiator in its lowered position the starting handle could no longer connect through to the engine. The radiator was in the way. To overcome this little difficulty a hole had been cut in the radiator to allow the handle to pass through it. The radiator cooling system relied on natural circulation as there was no circulating pump. So blanking off a section of the radiator effectively nullified about 25% of the radiator thereby reducing its cooling efficiency considerably. As a consequence Droopy's engine ran rather hot and it frequently boiled over. The radiator cap was not a tight fit, which may have been a good thing as it acted as a safety-valve. With the cap fitting so loosely it prevented the radiator from becoming a pressure vessel, one without some sort of release button. The driver and passenger often had to contend with steam and piping-hot droplets spraying back from the leaky cap.

The radiator itself was always leaking a little, especially around the hole made for the starting handle. A botched up attempt had been made to seal this area but it had obviously, never worked satisfactorily. The car was always thirsty and though I tried to cure the leaks with "Rad-Seal" several times, it helped a bit but it never succeeded in curing the problem completely.

"A Lesson in Overhauling an Engine"

John lived next door. He made his appearance on the scene with considerable eager enthusiasm. He was tall and rather thin and was about forty years old. As he was much older than I, I naturally assumed that he knew all about cars. He did give that impression. He took a great interest in Droopy-Drawers and after he had examined her thoroughly, tried the engine and by winding the starting-handle he could feel little resistance so he declared, with the confidence of an expert, that there was no doubt that the engine lacked compression.

"Well," I thought, "John ought to know." He was something in engineering; a scientist in fact, as he worked at the nearby Fort Halstead military research establishment, or so he claimed. He was himself, the proud owner of an ancient Austin 10 which was tucked away in his garage and which he had great plans for, so he said. John was also very eccentric and extremely highly-strung. His eyes fixed you with a terrifying stare and any relationship with him had to be very delicately handled. Arguing with John was out of the question and I have to admit, I was a bit scared of him.

John assured me with great authority that a new set of oversized piston-rings would cure the problem. In fact he said that they were essential. He also said that if I obtained all the necessary parts he would help me carry out the operation. We made a list. His assurance gave me confidence and I went ahead and bought all that was needed. I had to admit that the power of Droopy's engine was in no way related to the amount of noise it generated. It gave the impression, when driven, of being quite gutless; thus her nickname was coined; for she really needed stronger elastic.

When John had first brought his car home I was treated to a demonstration ride around the locality. I sat in the back in a compartment called the "dickie" seat. It was a seat within the boot. The seat was upholstered in padded, but rather worn, leather, as likewise was the boot lid that acted as a backrest. We went out for a demonstration drive and as we bowled along the floor of the boot suddenly gave way and I was left dangling and clutching the front of the "dickie" hanging on for grim death. John was completely unaware of my predicament and drove on loudly singing his heart out. I looked down at my dangling feet and I was horrified to see the road speeding beneath me.

Since the outing John's Austin 10 had gone into his garage for some minor attention, some routine maintenance, but had never made a re-appearance, indicating that something might be up. But, being young and naive I had never thought to ask myself this question. I rather naturally assumed that John knew what he was about and perhaps I could learn a thing or two from him.

That much was certainly true.

"A Bit of D. I. Y."

True to his word John came eagerly round one evening to help me. Rather, he took over and cheerfully stripped the engine down – completely! He came round to our house several evenings in succession after returning home from his work. It seemed he could not wait to get his hands dirty. We worked on the car under cover in my father's garage. There were bits and pieces, of car parts, everywhere; they littered the garage. I set about cleaning them up, scraping off carbon deposits and cleaning out the carburetor. I ground the valves and their seats and cleaned the points on the distributor, and so on. Many pieces including the heavy cast-iron engine block were laying on the workbench. One evening we were both beavering away when, all of a sudden, John abruptly turned round from the bench, rubbing his hands on a piece of oily rag and said cheerfully, but to my utmost horror, "Right then, Ted, I think I've got you started. I'll leave you to finish her off."

I tried not to show my shock. John brushed past me and went abruptly out of the garage; he hopped over the chestnut paling that divided our gardens and was gone. I was flabbergasted and didn't know what to do. I was utterly horrified and gazed stupidly at all the bits and pieces spread over the garage floor and workbench. Panic began to take hold but in the end there was nothing I could do but to get on with the job. I would just have to have a go at putting everything back together again. I had no other option.

John made no further appearances. He had never been very approachable as a person and it was impossible for me to go back to him. He had gone into hibernation. Everything, I realised, had to be worked out by myself, as there was no instruction book to go by. Carefully and gradually I got all the engine pieces back together again with help from a friend or two and the odd interested observer. Often, in the background, I could hear John practicing on his piano in his living room with the windows wide open and it was clear that he was struggling, hammering hard on the keyboard, trying to master a piece of complex, classical music.

Eventually the day came when I had everything in place and there was nothing further to do. I was under pressure from my father to vacate the garage. He wanted the use of it and was getting rather impatient. So at the point when I thought I should try out Droopy I gently eased her out of the garage onto the drive. It was a very critical moment for me because if the engine would not start then I could not imagine what there was left to try. I had done everything that I could possibly think of. I stood for a while almost frozen to the spot, wondering what I should do? There was nothing else for it, but to grasp the nettle, and so I got hold of the starting-handle and pushed it gingerly through the hole in the radiator. Fortunately there was no one about. No eyes of a cynical audience waiting to mock me and snigger if nothing happened. I paused and thought for a while frightened to give the handle a turn. I looked around again to make sure no one was watching, then I grasped the handle and quite casually gave it a swing. I got a shock for an unexpected and most extraordinary thing happened. The engine burst into life and then settled down to a healthy friendly purring note ticking over beautifully. I could not believe my luck. I was positively gob-smacked. I was absolutely elated. She had started first time, with just one swing of the handle; I could have hugged her. The engine chortled and idled away perfectly. It was like a dream come true though it was difficult to accept that a sort of miracle had occurred!

As I stood there almost frozen to the spot, at that very moment I looked up and saw John walking up his garden path towards me. He raised his right arm high in the air and gave me a thumbs-up sign. I began to wonder whether or not he had left me on purpose. Whatever, he had done me a great service as I had very quickly learned such a lot about cars. There was nothing in that car engine that I had not taken apart and put together again.

Although I did not know it at the time, John was a sick man. His behaviour became more erratic and eccentric. He died, poor chap, not long after from a tumor on the brain.

After all that I liked to believe that the engine had acquired a bit more power but it also had generated another problem: a slipping clutch. So my next task was to replace the clutch-plate and in doing so I had not entirely solved that problem either. I had bought a new set of toggle-levers, which operated the clutch thinking that might solve everything, but I was back to that one fundamental problem. The clutch pedal was mounted on the common transverse tube as the steering wheel and its operation had been similarly affected by that tube's angle change. I cannot remember how I solved the problem but I do remember that it had not been easy especially as I discovered that the previous owner had tampered with the mechanism in such a way as to make it very much worse. The new parts I had bought did not fit and had to be modified or doctored with the help of a lot of filing. Great determination was necessary to get the system to function at all. Solving one problem just exposed another.

So what had I achieved by buying Droopy? I had learned a lot about car maintenance from her which would be a great help for me in the future and it also taught me to be much more careful when buying a car in the future. She was a fun car and I was probably the envy of many who had no idea of the problems that were associated with her. Nor what trauma I had been going through. One should remember never judge anything in life by looks alone. Nothing is as it seems especially when it comes to cars. The headlamps though, were something else, they were superb. They were my favourite boast at that time. "They are so powerful," I would claim, "that when I drive down a country lane on full beam they singed the hedgerows!"

I got a sudden introduction into another one of Droopy's alarming idiosyncrasies one day when I turned sharp right into our lane. I had made one of my showy gear changes with a brisk bit of over accentuated revs to facilitate dropping down into a lower gear, when the accelerator pedal jammed in the down position, i.e.: at full throttle, and consequently the engine revs remained excessively high forcing me to turn the corner at a much faster pace than I had intended, or was wise. I quickly found that by wiggling my toe under the pedal I could yank it back up again, but it required very quick reactions and had to be done speedily in order to avoid a disaster. Her irascible nature was already beginning to show and I was beginning to feel that I could not wholly trust the little beast.

The rear suspension was also a little weak and so I fitted a pair of coil springs to beef it up. Some of the other problems were never properly overcome but in the end she was running quite well and I drove cheerfully round the Kent countryside for many a mile. Stopping her when necessary was still quite a problem though.

"A Red Coat"

SEEING RED

One day Droopy carried me over to Bletchingly, which is near Godstone in Surrey, to visit my old pal Barry. Barry and I had met when we were serving in the RAF doing our National-Service (which was obligatory in those days). We had both worked on the same aircraft, he as an airframe fitter and I as an engine mechanic. Barry's father owned a firm whose business was precision engineering. It was largely a family run business. Much of their trade was making units and parts for the petroleum industry; at this particular time they were fabricating some parts for 'Esso'. Barry told me that they had some 'Esso-red' paint left over and he thought that Droopy Drawers would look good if it were to be painted red.

He was very persistent and although I was hesitant at first, I had so much confidence in him, and that he would know exactly what he was doing that I was eventually persuaded to give him his head and let go him get on with it. Even then, I was quite nervous about the how the end result would look. After all, it could all go wrong.

Barry was not just a very competent engineer, but he was a fast worker too. We moved Droopy into the paint shop and he set to work. He was soon using the company's spray gun and leftover paint from Esso. Before long Droopy was transformed into her new shiny bright red livery. She took on a more 'go-faster' appearance than she had had before. Barry was a very handy person to know, and he did not stop there. As Droopy was inclined to overheat I asked him if he could cut a series of holes on both sides of the bonnet. I had bought some chromium-plated draw-pulls so that they fitted exactly over the holes like a form of fluting. The idea was to improve the air circulation under the bonnet and to add to the appearance of the car. It may have made some difference in the case of the latter but not much to the former.

It is not every day that someone leaves home in a car coloured British Racing Green, only to return home on the same day, in the same car, in bright Fire-engine red.

Good old Barry also made a tubular frame to support the hood. It was designed as an inverted 'U' shape or a goal-post confighuration, which dropped into matching tubes we had fitted onto the car's bodywork. This frame was made to split into two parts so that it could be easily taken apart and stored. My mother made a hood to fit over the frame and took advantage of the press-studs which were already there in position, and which also served to hold the 'tonneau-cover' in place.

I went on a journey down to Cornwall with some of the lads I knew, we traveled in a convoy of Austin Sevens and Barry came along on his Matchless motorbike. We were camping but the weather was awful so we stayed the last two nights in a disused coast-guards' cottage before we gave up and went home. This was Droopy's first long tour and no serious problems were encountered, this gave me confidence in her reliability.

Some fifty years have past since these events and many details are now long forgotten. However, I feel I ought to remember from where, or from whom, I obtained a super brass hooter, but I can't. Some kind soul gave it to me. It was large, made of shiny brass with a large rubber bulb, which when squeezed: emitted a wonderful sound, "Barp-barp, Barp-barp." Now I really did feel like Mr. Toad! Barp-barp, Barp-barp ~ terrific! I mounted it on the outside of the car within easy reach of the driver's right hand. It was louder than the klaxon but I often used the two together. "Barp-barp, Barp-barp", and when I pressed the two audible signals together: - "Err-er-Err; Barp-barp" it certainly attracted the attention of the general public, who seemed to greatly enjoy the performance. They brought the house down!

I also went on a few treasure hunts, some of which were organised by the Young Conservatives. There were no prizes for those who came in first with all questions answered. John Hall, my friend who navigated and I were a good combination. With Droopy it was easy to pass all the driving skill tests that were set at various stages along the route and somehow or other between us, we managed to get most of the questions right. We always arrived at the destination ages before anyone else!

Another embarrassing adventure sticks in my mind. One day, as usual, I drove Droopy into the Borough Green Station car park before catching the train to London. Cars were parked at right-angles to the hilly station approach. Luckily I managed to procure one of these favoured parking places. One of these parking-bays was the best spot from where one could make a quick getaway at night in the rush-hour traffic. The downside was that if one did not get out of the train a bit sharpish and make a rapid dash for the exit, then the main throng of vehicles queuing to leave the car park would box one in. In such a situation, one had to wait until the off-chance of a gracious driver holding back the traffic stream and beckoning you to leave before him. However that only happened on the rarest of occasions.

On this particular evening I had done well to get out of the station before anybody else. I sprinted to my car, and I jumped in (having by this time become quite adept at fitting my long legs under the steering wheel). I pressed the starter-button and good old Droopy fired up immediately. We started to move briskly out of the parking bay with the intention of making a quick get-away, BUT, Droopy stopped suddenly, having stalled after moving only a few feet. Droopy and I were now blocking the path of the other cars coming up the slope. How embarrassing. I started her up again but the same thing happened. She stalled a second time! I checked everything, even the handbrake, started her up – and she stalled again! By this time I was acutely embarrassed and extremely puzzled. I was at a loss to know what to do.

Out of the first car that I had caused to stop, and which I was obstructing, stepped a giant of a man with a bushy beard and wearing a wide brimmed bush-hat, which added to his fearsome image. He walked slowly up to the side of the car, looked down on me and said quietly and slowly, clearly enunciating his words through his teeth, "You – are - tied - to – a - tree." With that he turned and walked back to his own car.

By this time, all hot and bothered, I jumped out of the car puzzling over what he meant. It became all too obvious when I got out and went round the to look at the back of the car. There was a row of sycamore trees at the side of the parking spaces and there I saw the answer: - a hefty rope was tied to one of these trees and the other end was attached to Droopy's spare-wheel. Fortunately it did not take long for me to untie the rope. As I got into the car I waved to the bearded man a polite 'thank-you' who had been waiting without showing any sign of impatience. Not so the other commuters; they were hooting and standing by their open car doors trying to see what was holding up their exit.

This experience made me much more cautious.   I became wary when parking near trees. No damage had been done to the car, fortunately. Had Droopy had a little more 'go' in her, then a strong rope like that might have caused a lot more trouble and done some damage.

I did wonder whether the miscreant(s), who had tied the car to the tree, had been lurking hiding somewhere to witness the result of their mischievous prank. Despite the embarrassment and frustration their action had caused me, I had a certain admiration for their idea.   The thought crossed my mind that it was the sort of trick that I would have liked to play on some poor unsuspecting innocent motorist myself.

Part 2

"The Continent Beckons"

About this time another friend of mine, one Mike Jarrett, had invited me to go on a sailing trip in the English Channel, from Dover, in his parents yacht with his father in charge. This turned out to be an adventure full of drama and excitement, but that is another story. After that episode I wondered how I could return the favour. I came up with the idea of touring the continent in Droopy (of course) staying in camping sites. On the sailing trip we had crossed the channel, calling in at Calais. It was my first taste of being abroad, and a very brief one at that, but it was long enough to wet my appetite for foreign travel. Since that trip I had applied for a passport in case the possibility of going abroad presented itself again, well one never knows. In a way I was ready for more adventure and to give impetus to the idea there was the U.S. army bivouac tent and a simple methylated spirit stove gathering dust and waiting to be used in our garage! Mike took the bait and agreed to come along.

Once again, because it was so long ago I cannot remember all the details involved in planning the trip but I do remember booking the ferry and arranging the 'AA' 5 star insurance cover for travelling abroad. The "AA" 's head-office wasn't very far away, so I popped down to Fanum House, their HQ, which was situated on London Road, on our side of Maidstone. We were ill prepared. We made no plans at all. We had no particular destination in mind. Nor did we carry out any research for any particular route we might take. The trip was a bit of a spur-of-the-moment decision made by a rather headstrong young man; i.e.: me.

We loaded up the car the night before our departure. The luggage space behind the seat's backrest was rather restricted, so most of our luggage had to be strapped on top of the back of the car, which proved to be most inconvenient if only because that was where the petrol filler cap was situated, and every time we wanted to refuel, all the luggage would have to come off to get at the fuel tank's cap. What is more; Droopy did not have a fuel gauge. All I had to indicate the state of the petrol was a brass rod, which would measure the depth of the fuel by dipping it into the tank. It was a simple dipstick and if I thought I was running out of fuel I had to use it to get confirmation. It would be a nuisance to say the least, as one can imagine. We guestimated how much fuel we had used, by the miles travelled.

We set off full of anticipation. On the way to Dover where we were to catch the ferry it started to rain hard. The rain increased in intensity the nearer we got towards the coast. We had assembled the hood cover which offered us some protection from above, but still the rain would wet us from the unprotected sides. We had dispensed with the side windows, as they were almost opaque Perspex and were useless against any rain. The solitary small windscreen wiper-blade worked by a suction pump, which was connected by a small, bore rubber tube to the inlet manifold on the engine and the amount of suction was influenced by how hard the engine was working. Fortunately, on the early part of the drive on the A20 to Dover, the hills were not too steep and so the wiper was not affected unduly by a tough climb and a labouring engine, but when we got to Folkestone we had to tackle the infamous Dover Hill (on the old A20) out of Folkestone. With the engine working harder and harder going up-hill the windscreen-wiper would go slower and slower, and it could come to a stop. Sometimes I could make it sweep more quickly by blipping the engine but on the Dover Hill it stopped altogether. I had to lean right out of the side window so that I could see around the windscreen to try and get a view of the road ahead. By this time we were driving pretty slowly so that was not quite as serious as it might have been. The water in the radiator was just about to boil by the time we got to the top. Once over the top and on the downward slope into Dover the single little wiper-blade thrashed wildly threatening to damage itself.

We had a long wait for the ferry in Dover and while we were in the queue of cars waiting to load I was sitting of the weather side in a puddle of water and I was freezing and I don't think Mike was much warmer. Ferries ran less frequently in those days and they were much smaller vessels. They were not fitted with stabilisers and any facilities they provided for passengers were very basic. These were the days before the roll-on-roll-off ferries and no one was allowed to drive their own car onto the lower deck of the ship. The crew attended to that for you. By the time we got on board the 'Lord Warden' we were wet and very cold and feeling generally most uncomfortable. We searched around for somewhere warm and found it by standing with our backs to the funnel and facing the sunny side. By the time we had reached Calais we had almost dried out and we were feeling a lot warmer.

All foot and car passengers disembarked but those with cars had to wait on the quayside for their vehicle to be driven off by a member of the crew and for it to be handed back. It was a time consuming exercise. One by one the cars emerged and then suddenly the flow stopped. Perhaps one had failed to start or there had been a collision, and we waited patiently. Everyone was leaning over the handrail watching and waiting for the appearance of their particular vehicle, including us. We were all becoming restless after a long period with nothing happening. Eventually a member of the crew emerged from the car deck, stood with his hands on hips and then he cupped his hands round his mouth.

And shouted: "Who owns the red Austin 7?"

I raised my hand grinning with embarrassment.

"Oh it's you. How do you start the bloody thing?"

"There's a button under the dashboard." I shouted back.

He turned tail and strode steadily back into the bowels of the ship. We waited but still there was no sign of Droopy or any other car. Another crewmember eventually appeared.

"Oi," he yelled, "come with me!" "We can't start your bloody car!"

So I had to make my way down and around to the car deck then follow the crew-man to where Droopy was parked, right on the bend. The cars were driven in forwards and then each one had to be turned around in order to be driven out again. I imagined Droopy was quite pleased to see me. It was so dark on the car deck and very dismal. She was surrounded by half a dozen or so crewmen in their navy blue overalls. I jumped into the driver's seat and soon had her engine running and was relieved that nothing was wrong and that she started so easily. The steel hollow car deck made an ideal sound box and amplified the throaty roar of the engine. With several loud bursts as I blipped the throttle, I drove out into the sunshine to be greeted by good humoured friendly cheers, clapping and waving from the passengers who were still waiting patiently for their vehicles.

I picked up Mike and we went through the French Customs who removed the first page of the Triptyque, which I had obtained to enable us to take our car through national borders legally. It was a temporary import/export document, which I had obtained through the auspices of the 'AA'. One page of the document had to be torn out and handed over to customs as one entered a country. The driver of the vehicle kept the second copy and a third was removed by customs when one left that country. One had to go through this performance at every national border as one drove through the Continent and as we had made no plans, we did not know in advance how many times we would have to do this. And of course each nation has its own currency, there were no nice and simple Euros in those days.

"Tea Break"

EN LA FRANCE

The beginning of the Breakdowns, No. 1

Our first shock once we drove away from the harbour, was the dreadful condition of the roads. They were far worse than anything we had driven on in England. We certainly had not anticipated poor road surfaces. It simply had not entered our heads that there would be such a state of affairs and that it could be such a worry to us, where Droopy was concerned. The roads were rich in uneven cobbles and potholes, accompanied in many instances with a pronounced camber. They were dreadful to put it mildly. English roads by comparison were like billiard tables. Poor Droopy was really suffering especially with carrying the extra weight of our camping equipment and luggage strapped to her back. The Austin 7 suspension was not good at the best of times and my little Austin's suspension was even poorer than compared to the standard car. Droopy had a rather narrow wheelbase and where the situation allowed, I drove her along the footpath, on which the surface tended to be much better. It went some way to ease her pain and suffering. In addition to that without any direction indicators both of us had to be very alert, as travelling on the continent and driving on the right required the passenger to give most of the hand signals.

The weather cleared in those first few hours and it became warm. We assumed that Droopy had lost some water en route from Dover and in addition the shaking on the cobbles must have done nothing for her poorly sealed radiator and connections. Her engine boiled and we came to a necessary halt near Cassel. When Droopy had cooled down enough for me to remove the radiator cap, I checked the water level only to find no water visible at all. The radiator was empty. So leaving Mike by the car, I walked along the road until I came to a cottage, knocked on the door and in my limited schoolboy French I asked the old lady who opened it for some water.

"Du vin?" asked the old lady quizzically.

"Non. Du l'eau, s'il vous plait". I replied.

"De la biere?" she asked again.

"Non, non, l'eau, s'il vous plait". I pointed to the bottle in my hand.

"Vous etes Anglais?"

"Er, mais oui, Madame".

"Un moment". With such a look of understanding she disappeared inside the cottage with the bottle.

After quite some time she reappeared and smiling proudly presented me with my bottle. It felt very warm, almost hot, and it was full of a brown liquid. I examined the contents and looked back at the lady with raised eyebrows.

"Thé Anglais" She nodded and smiled and repeated the word "Thé" pointing at the bottle. I immediately realised why she had taken so long to fetch a simple bottle of water. She had, of course, been full of good intentions and was very kind in her own way having gone through a lot of extra trouble but it was not 'Thé' that was needed. I thanked her profusely and walked back to Mike with the bottle of tea and full of embarrassment handed him the bottle. He looked perplexed.

"What have you got there?" he asked.

"Tea", I said not looking at him.

"Tea", cried Mike. "You went to fetch bleedin' water! That should have been a simple enough task surely".

"Yes, well I know that, but as tea goes it is not very strong and fortunately it does not have any milk in it", I explained.

Poor Mike was neither impressed nor pleased. As there were no other houses within sight and as we needed the water desperately, after some debate we decided to pour the tea into the radiator. It served as a good "pick-me-up" as it kept Droopy going for the rest of that day.

Our first breakdown, she had run out of water, and had
to make do with tea.

"A lucky Break"

Breakdown No. 2

As we drove towards and then through Lille over severely
bumpy roads, Droopy's engine began to sound very rough.
I brought the car to a halt and opened the bonnet to try to
determine what was wrong. It did not take long for us to
diagnose the problem. It was simple. One sparking-plug
lead was missing! Droopy was running only on three
cylinders, hence the worrying noise. We felt that we could
not continue as things were and I suggested to Mike that if
I walked back into the town maybe I could find a garage
that might have a re-placement lead. We removed another
plug lead for me to use as a sample. Mike stayed on guard
by the car while I set off along a busy main road towards
the town feeling pretty depressed and was not at all
confident that I would get a new sparking plug lead even if
I did find a garage. As I passed a particularly complicated
road junction I noticed something lying in the middle of
the road right amongst the moving traffic. It looked very
much like the missing plug lead and even if it was not
Droopy's, perhaps it could be adapted to fit. From where I
stood it seemed to be of similar proportions, or that was
what I bemusedly thought and which gave me a grain of
hope. It was certainly worth investigating, so biding my
time, I began to calculate when it would be safe for me to
rush out into the traffic stream and snatch up the object. At
that moment it seemed to me to be a matter of life and
death in more ways than one. Getting that plug-lead was as
equally important as looking after my own skin. I made a
rather foolhardy dash into the traffic, when there seemed
to be a lull and a slightly larger gap between the vehicles.
So skipping and dodging the irate and hooting drivers I
zoomed in on that one small, but important piece lying
there on the ground hoping to retrieve it as safely and
quickly as possible. To scoop up the lead would be a

difficult action as I had to take my eyes off the traffic as I did so, then spin round and scamper back to the safety of the pavement.

The treasure that I had risked life and limb for looked to me suspiciously like Droopy's own plug lead. The more I examined it the more convinced I became, though at the same time it was not quite the wonderful turn of events I had first thought. The fitting on the end of the lead that screwed into the distributor head had been crushed under the wheels of many cars. Fortunately, I saw a garage ahead and walked quickly towards it. I went into the forecourt and finding several garage workers tried to explain my problem, but all I got was a shake of the head and a shrug of the shoulders. I suppose this reaction was hardly surprising as the garage only sold petrol and was not in the business of carrying out repairs. A man with a scooter had been watching me quizzically from a distance. He left his machine and came over to enquire the nature of my problem using sign language. He eagerly persuaded me to give him the broken plug lead. Trustingly I gave him both the broken one and the good one, although I was a bit hesitant. By pointing at his watch and with a few more signs I gathered that he would be back in ten minutes. He mounted his scooter and puttered off weaving in and out of the traffic leaving a haze of blue smoke behind him and I watched him, and my plug leads, rapidly disappear from sight. I was feeling very anxious. Those plug leads had better come back, or we would be in serious trouble. Ten minutes went by, then twenty and still no sign of the young man on the scooter. Half an hour ticked away and by this time I was beginning to panic. With only two sound plug-leads left there was no possibility of Droopy moving and it also meant that I had lost the sample lead that I would need to find replacements. Forty minutes went by and still there was no re-appearance of the young man and his scooter. I was just about to go back to the car to remove the third lead to use as a sample and go myself to look for another garage when I heard a most welcome sound. It was the pop, pop, pop of the scooter. He came to a stop beside me and triumphantly held up a handful of spark plug leads, which he had been clutching. He did not get off his scooter but stretched out his hand and passed over the entire bundle to me. Then with a wave of goodbye he drove off with a pop, pop, pop followed by a haze of blue smoke, never to be seen by me again. I had not paid him. I had not had time to thank him; he was just the first of several 'Guardian-angels' we were to meet on our trip.

Mike and I eagerly examined the bunch of leads and found not only Droopy's sample one and the crushed one but also a new one of exactly the same type. It did not take long to get the plug leads fitted and to get the engine going again, producing a healthy sounding engine note once more.

Thank goodness we were back in business.

"Breaking up"

Breakdown No. 3

So on we went. The rough roads, often cobbled, which we thought could almost be classified as boulders, were punishing our poor fragile little car. We watched with envy at the busy little Citroen 2CVs (a little car with great character), as they rode effortlessly over the cobbles. Their wheels flopped about as if they were mounted on rubber. Their suspension was obviously designed to cope with the continental roads. Droopy's certainly was not, and she shook and vibrated until we became quite worried. It was not long before the off-side wheel's mudguard stay-bolt broke.

The mudguards had originally been designed and intended to be fitted to motorcycles, which would have the support of the machines forks and a stay on each side of the mudguard and wheel. But in Droopy's case there was only one stay mounted separate from the body of the car, and it was only possible to have one stay per mudguard. That one was mounted on the wheel's back-plate, so that everything turned in unison with each front wheel. It would have been a simple job to replace the bolt except that the bolt in question went through the plate which carried the brake shoes. And that meant that the brakes had to be completely dismantled to access the bolt and to fit a replacement. As an amazing bit of good fortune, in amongst my tools and bits and pieces I just happened to have a spare bolt complete with nut and locking-washer which suited the purpose exactly. As I had changed the brake shoes once before I knew what to do, but in that case it had not been done at the roadside or in the middle of the open countryside. The relevant wheel had to be removed, and whilst I was struggling to tighten the stay bolt firmly I must have exerted too much pressure and Droopy suddenly fell off the jack. The jack was caught under the car, trapped by the undercarriage and thereby irretrievable. It seemed an insoluble predicament.

However, not to be outdone, nor give up, I went off into the nearby wood in search of a long wooden pole, possibly a fence pole. As luck would have it, I found what I wanted and returned to the car and to Mike. He was pretty dejected at this stage, his confidence in Droopy, and me, was ebbing away fast. I laid the loose front wheel at a convenient point on the ground close to the front hub and used that to provide a fulcrum for the pole, which I then used as a lever. By that means I managed to raise the front of the car sufficiently for Mike to edge out the trapped jack from under the car and hope and pray that it did not slip and fall on him whilst he did so. So all was not lost. The jack was back in use, and the full repair was finally completed.

We had blackened and greasy hands which we managed to get only slightly clean by rubbing them together with sand and dust gleaned from the roadside. It was a dry summer, and we had very limited reserves of water. We needed to conserve what water we had in case Droopy was thirsty and so we could top up her radiator.

So we were looking rather grubby, as we continued on our way once more.

"Breaking point?"

POINT DUTY

Traffic lights were few and far between in those days in Britain and on the Continent. I think it was in Lille that we came upon a large and busy complex road junction. In the centre of which, and in the midst of the madly careering, hither and dithering of traffic, stood a podium. This podium was like an island, which was occupied by a dashing looking gendarme. Vehicles were crisscrossing the junction in all directions.

And Droopy's klaxon went:—
"Er-Er Errr".

It was a noisy and chaotic scene, but it also seemed to be very much under the control of an efficient gesticulating gendarme. Whilst we waited for our turn to be allowed to proceed across this turmoil, we gazed in admiration as he waved his arms about, making dramatic gestures as if he was conducting an orchestra. Pointing this way and that at individual cars with his baton, his every gesture was punctuated by accompanying shrill blasts on his whistle. He was fascinating to watch, but the only problem was that it appeared to us that we were being ignored. It may have been that we were unable to interpret his signals but nonetheless we were waiting at the edge of this circus for what seemed to us to be a very long time. I waited a while longer but suddenly, out of devilment perhaps, I blasted away on Droopy's big brass hooter: Barp, Barp, and then pressed the klaxon just for good measure. The policeman could not help but hear us. Startled, he spun round briskly on his podium until he caught sight of us. I gave another blast on the hooter at which he fell about laughing nearly falling off his podium. He gathered himself together and with dramatic sweeping gestures he graciously beckoned me to drive forward across his junction, or so I interpreted his meaning. But as I did so, I suddenly had to swerve sharply in order to avoid colliding with another car. It was a very close shave. Immediately there was a shrill blast on the whistle, then with another blast the policeman raised his baton, his arm erect and pointing skywards above his head. All the traffic stopped as if petrified. With his free arm he pointed directly and firmly at the car with which I had nearly collided. Then he sprung down from his podium and strode purposefully over to the driver pointing his baton hard at him. There was a brief exchange between the two, which resulted in the poor man being issued with a ticket. Which the gendarme executed with a flourish. Having done his duty he waved us on our way with a broad smile and a polite exaggerated bow, a salute and a nod. He then nipped back up onto his podium to carry on with his work. The road junction was his stage and he was the director. One could imagine him as a graceful bullfighter with his cloak and his movements. Instead of a bull, he was playing with, and manipulating, dashing cars all of them in his ring at one and the same time.

We continued on our way until we came to the Belgium Border and the Customs Post. Once again we showed our passports, and surrendered the relevant pages of the Triptyque as we left France and entered Belgium, our second country of that day. We headed towards Brussels, but the evening was closing in and we needed to find somewhere to stay the night. In Flobecq we found a very rough and ready camp on a small site at the back of a cheap run-down little transport-café. The rather plump, solemn, woman proprietor wearing an apron offered us the opportunity to sleep in the back of the remains of a large rusty old van.

That would save us the bother of pitching our tent, she might have looked a bit severe but she thought kindly enough. She then told us we would be sharing this "luxury accommodation" with two German boys. This was the first time we had spent the night on our own abroad and the prospect of sharing accommodation with two German youths wearing lederhosen, did not appeal to us at all, probably influenced by having seen so many wartime newsreels. However I felt we could not easily refuse the lady's hospitality, as she seemed to be well meaning, very friendly, and with a nice nature. I was really worried that we would not survive the night. But we must have got off to sleep eventually and we slept soundly. When we woke up in the morning, we were rather surprised to find that nothing untoward had happened to us during the night. The Germans seemed to be quiet and unassuming sort of fellows, surprisingly likeable and friendly; not at all threatening, and not at all what we envisaged Germans to be.

The two German boys

"Breakthrough"

RED LIGHT IN LIEGE

The next day we found ourselves bang in the centre of Brussels. We parked the car and had a look around the main square, found the Manneken-Pis, as all tourists must and then we were off again.

We were not quite sure where we were going because we could not seem to find Liege nor Luik, which, from our map, was where we thought we might want to visit and make our next destination. Only somewhere called Luttik seemed to be what was prominently displayed on all the signposts, and there was no sign of Liege at all. As we had no specific plans we supposed Luik or even Luttik might do just as well as any other town; it was all a new experience to us. This time we camped on a proper campsite at Juppile, close to the big town of Luik and it gradually dawned on us that Luik, Luttik and Luttich were all one and the same place and as for the Liege that appeared on our English map, well that was the same place too!

Having established our pitch, it was rather a hot night, so before turning in we decided to venture into the town to do a bit of evening sightseeing. We decided to head off first towards the cathedral, which was a good landmark, and which we could clearly see in the distance. To our surprise on nearing the cathedral, we were accosted by a lot of girls who grabbed us by our arms and tried to divert us physically into the doorways of premises that lined each side of the road. No sooner had we shaken one lot off then we were greeted or accosted in a similar manner by more persistent, friendly maidens. A fellow called out *"English, come, we show you nice girls, very nice girl. You 'ave a good time, no?"* Then men dressed like doormen in grey suits and peaked hats called out, *"ey, nice girls for you.*

Give you good time, you like?" This was a totally new and unexpected experience for us innocents abroad. We were very uncomfortable, embarrassed and rather scared. We ran the gauntlet along this street until we got to the cathedral. I don't think even then had we fully realised that we had just passed through a 'red light district'. Was this why it was known as the "city of fire"? I do not think that either of us then was aware that such places existed. We mulled over our experience with some concern while we were going round the cathedral and I suppose that between us we put two and two together and started to realise that we had, in fact, strayed into the Red Light District. That it was situated so close to the cathedral, we thought, was absolutely scandalous. It was very handy for the clergy, though, we mused.

Then we had a discussion about returning to the campsite. We had no map of the town and no-where to get a town plan for tourists as Information Offices were non-existent in those days, and even had they been, they would more than likely have been closed at the end of the working day. The only way we could find our way back to the campsite was to retrace our steps, but that would mean that we would have to make our way through gauntlet again, and brave the "sirens". After some deliberation we decided on a plan which was to walk back down the road with a determined and steady gait, looking dead ahead expressionless and ignore any advances, and this was exactly what we did, as a result we were hardly bothered at all.

"One lives and learns".

Driving on the right meant that the passenger on the left had to take on the role of making the necessary hand signals when required.

"Breaking into smiles"

ON INTO GERMANY

The next morning promised to grow into another very hot day. We were having more confusion over our map reading and navigation: "Just where was 'Aix-la-Chapelle'?" we asked ourselves. All the road signs seemed to be pointing to this place, but we could not identify it on our map. The puzzle to us was, that there appeared to be no signs at all to the Aachen that we were trying to head for. Eventually we arrived at another national border and customs posts at which we had to go through all the formalities again to be able to leave Belgium. Our passports had to be stamped and we had to complete the triptyque for the car. Having done so, we made our way across to the German Zoll offices a hundred yards or so ahead. And of course, we had to switch currency again, this time from Belgium Francs to German Marks. What a pain! And each time there was commission deducted.

At the customs control I was immediately apprehensive at the sight of the German military style grey uniforms. The war was not so many years behind us. We nervously went into the customs office to attend to the business of passport stamping and the cumbersome triptyque process. The customs officers looked to me just like some enemy soldiers out of a WW2 war film. I did not like the look of them at all and was definitely rather worried. However, the officers were all smiles and laughter and as I had not expected that, the whole scenario seemed a little unsettling to me. Their friendly attitude was the reverse of what I had anticipated especially as at all the other custom border posts we had passed through, the Belgium and French officers manning them had been pokerfaced and taken their business very seriously. On the counter of the German Customs office stood a birdcage, in which was a canary. I happened to look at this with some curiosity and

I probably wore a puzzled expression. One of the customs officers must have noticed this and rushed up to explain, "Unser einziger Gefangner" ("Our only prisoner" he explained jokingly). They certainly had a sense of humour and we joined in the mirth, everyone was all smiles. These friendly officials were, to me, completely out of character. Then, believe it or not, they all trooped out of their office to admire our car parked outside, and as we made our departure there was quite a cheerful gathering to wave us off. We did not mind in the least but it was totally unexpected, and not a little puzzling.

As the day wore on it became very hot and we were worried because Droopy was losing water so much we had difficulty in keeping up with her thirst. We drove on and all of a sudden we realised that 'Aachen' was appearing on the signposts. That was what we had been looking for! We decided to go there after all and to Hell with Aix-la-Chapelle, which we now seemed to have lost. 'Aachen' was on our map so we knew exactly where we were heading for, and once there, we would know exactly where we were!

"Break off"

Breakdown No. 4

Eventually, the penny dropped. Aachen and Aix-la-Chapelle were one and the same place. We drove out of Aachen and were just heading out of town eastwards when we were forced to pull over. Droopy was seriously overheating and we found that there was no water whatsoever in the radiator and we had not got anymore with us. Upon further examination I discovered that the brackets, which held the radiator in place, had broken. The unrestrained radiator, therefore, was shaking and rattling about. It couldn't withstand much of that treatment. We realized that it was only the connecting hoses that were keeping it from falling out onto the road! We just could not carry on like this. We were standing by the roadside silently wondering what on earth we should do. We were extremely concerned, and whilst I was trying to think of some sort of solution, I happened to caste my gaze about me. I was very close to despair and wondering where I could get some water when I happened to notice, to my complete utter astonishment, that just across the road there was a company that specialised in radiators AND radiator repairs! They had a large billboard, which showed a picture of a leaking radiator. I could not believe it. Was it a mirage I was seeing? Was I dreaming? It was one of those extra-ordinary coincidences that one experiences very rarely in life. It was our salvation and I shouted excitedly to Mike.

"Do you see what I see, Mike?"

I pointed to the premises across the road. Mike agreed that it certainly looked as if it was a radiator repair shop. If he could see it as well me, then it could not be a mirage. It was nothing short of a miracle. We jumped into the car. Water or no water we drove the car a little way up the road, made a U-turn and returned eagerly down the other side of the road into the radiator repair premises, turning briskly into their yard. Sure enough, it was exactly what it declared itself to be. A Radiator Repair Workshop! There were radiators of all shapes and sizes stacked everywhere around the yard. There was no doubt. We had struck gold and felt that our guardian angel was working for us once more.

We did not know what sort of reception we would receive there so I ventured very gingerly into the workshop and found someone. He was a mechanic in overalls. I could only beckon with my hand as my German was far too weak for me to call him out to the car, or to explain to him what our predicament was. Mike had already opened up the bonnet to display the disaster, which with one glance, one could see was all too evident. The mechanic had a good look round the engine and especially around the damaged radiator at the same time muttering under his breath. Then he suddenly stood up and gesticulating with his hands in a display of helplessness as if the whole world was watching he exclaimed'

"Alles ist kaputt, alles ist kaputt".

With some difficulty we managed to come to an agreement that if we would take out the radiator he would then try to mend it. He was not happy, which he made very apparent by a lot of head shaking and shrugging of shoulders. He repeatedly muttered, "Meine Güte, mein Gott, alles ist kaputt. Alles ist kaputt".

We had no choice and were entirely in his hands and reliant on his skills. We did as he suggested and set about extricating the radiator from the car. This did not take that long and we were soon handing over the radiator to the mechanic.

He blocked off the radiator outlet by hammering home a solid rubber bung and then another special bung at the inlet, which had an air hose attached through it, to enable him to apply air pressure. He then immersed the pressurized radiator in a tank of water. And lots of bubbles appeared from many spots on the surface of the radiator especially around the hole that had been cut into it to accommodate the starting handle. The bubbles illustrated all too plainly that our radiator was absolutely rotten with leaks.

"Mein Gott, meine Güte" he kept muttering. "Donnerwetter!"

He pulled out the radiator from the water tank, blew the radiator dry with a compressed-air line and then placed it on the workbench. He then set earnestly to work. We watched him beat the radiator all round with a rubber hammer to seek out the weak points and then seal them by soldering, and he even adjusted the outlet pipe, which was set at an awkward angle. Because it looked ungainly he straightened it up, making it look a lot neater. The radiator was soon checked for leaks in the water tank and once he attached the mounting brackets it was ready to be replaced back in front of the engine. The radiator fitter had done a thorough job. Mike and I re-installed the radiator and fitted all the associated parts, filled it with water and closed the bonnet. Droopy looked herself again. It was going to be a relief not to worry about filling her up with water every few miles. From now on we could look forward to trouble free motoring. Or so we thought.

I cannot remember what the bill came to but I do recall that at the time we had considered it ridiculously cheap. We were very thankful for that. Time was getting on and we were feeling hungry. Most of the day had gone by without us having had a chance to get anything to eat or drink, not even so much as a cup of tea. The Proprietor from the radiator workshop had called his wife and family out for them to make our acquaintance and to wish us a genial goodbye, but what we all did not know then, was that we would soon be back!

Oh yes. Oh dear.

"Give us a break"

Breakdown No. 5

We now set off all ship shape and Bristol fashion, in a happier and more confident mood, to continue our interrupted journey in the knowledge that we now had a car at last with a watertight radiator. We were grateful for that. However we had only been going a couple of kilometres or so when tragedy struck! For some reason the car's engine had appeared to have become very hot, so we drew to a stop with a question in our minds. "How could that be possible?" we asked each other. I removed the radiator cap and saw to my horror that the radiator was completely dry.

Absolutely mystified I ferreted around and it was not long before I discovered the reason. The bottom circulating hose was cut through allowing all the water from the radiator to escape. After a while we worked out that the new corrugated flexible hose had been cut by the suspension's damper-arm. The damper was comprised of a pair of thin metal plates. They had acted like a pair of scissors. Anything that became tangled in them was cut in half, which for us spelt disaster. We realised that the fitter, with the best intentions, had repaired the radiator in such a way that to him was the only possible solution. He had **re-aligned** the outlet connection. Whilst that looked better, it had been a mistake. As he had altered it, only to re-connect the outlet pipe in such a way that it then passed through and between these two damper arm blades. So, when the car went over the prolific bumps the suspension was depressed enough for these arms to act like scissors and chop the bottom pipe in two. Thereby letting out all the cooling water. We were again in serious trouble and a long way from the radiator workshop. We were in a rural area that was remote from any type of garage or help.

Eventually, we decided to flag down a car to see if we could persuade someone to give us a tow back to the radiator repair workshop. Would anyone stop for us, that would be the question? I climbed a bank from where I would spot any vehicle that was approaching, and that seemed to be suitable for giving us a tow. Mike stayed down by the car to wait on a shout from me so that he could flag down the vehicle as it drew near. I was not on the bank for long before I spotted an English car heading our way.

'Quick, Mike', I yelled, hardly disguising my excitement. 'Here comes a British car. For Pete's sake stop it'.

I clambered down the bank to give him support. Thankfully the car stopped and I explained our predicament to the driver and his companion. They took some persuading, but they finally agreed to give us a tow. But of course, no-one had a towrope, but they did say that they had passed a filling station about half a kilometre down the road, which could possibly have a rope. I set off at a sprint to see whether I could beg, borrow or steal a towrope from the station. Despite my language shortcomings amazingly I manage to buy a rope for 10 DM and with an agreement that money would be refunded if and when I returned it ~ sale or return. I was quite pleased that I had managed to broker this deal, as in those days very few people spoke English, and I was additionally hampered by my feeble knowledge of German. I returned breathless to the car with the rope and Mike and I set about turning Droopy round to face the other way and to push her across the road. Fortunately Droopy was not that heavy to push but to get across a busy main road required time and patience. We succeeded in the end but were at the same time mindful of the fact that we were delaying our new-found English friends. Fortunately the way back to the radiator repair workshop was not too far. Our worry was that during the tow, if the car in front of us might have to make a sudden stop. Droopy's brakes might let us down. By arrangement we agreed that when we arrived at the workshop we would give a few Barp, barps on the hooter to let them know we were there. It was a conspicuous building so it was not too hard to identify. So stopping, as it turned out, was not too difficult an operation. On arrival we cast off the towrope and said our thanks and bade our Good Samaritans good-bye.

Mike and I pushed Droopy back into the radiator repair yard. Mr. Radiator Man appeared in the doorway of his workshop. He looked very perplexed and then became aghast with horror. He put his hands on his hips with a growing look of incredulity on his face. He was not pleased to see us again. By miming with hand signals and drawing a sketch on a piece of paper we manage to convey to him what had gone wrong with the radiator repair and what the problem was. He eventually realised that by his well-meaning re-alignment of the hose connection he had in fact caused the problem. There was nothing for it but to take the whole front of the car apart and extract the radiator once again. Mrs. Radiator Man came out into the yard with her brother who spoke some English. He shook our hands and explained that he had been a prisoner of the British in the last war and that they had treated him with great kindness. As he explained this, still holding my hand, tears welled up in his eyes. He bade us come into the house where they had a meal waiting for us. They must have realised that we had not eaten all day. We got ourselves cleaned up as best we could, as we were pretty dirty by then. In the kitchen a meal of cold meats, cheeses and bread was spread on the table. We ate while our radiator was being repaired out in the workshop and soon our hunger was appeased. The wife kept asking if we found the food nice and then brought in more. Her English brother had by this time had gone outside so we were unable to tell her that we had had enough.

"For Christ's sake tell her we have had enough" muttered Mike in desperation. I felt that she had been so kind as to bring the food that we should show willing and eat it. In the end we resorted to acting by clutching our stomachs and blowing out our cheeks to tell her we had had plenty.

Mr Radiator Man came into the kitchen wiping his hands on a rag and announced that the radiator was "Fertig". This time he was all smiles. It was almost evening so we quickly set about fitting the radiator back in place and re-assembling the front of the car. We could not thank the family enough and to our surprise they refused to take any more money. We bade our fond farewells to that wonderfully kind family in Julicher Strasse, and left Aachen behind. Once again we found that Germany was full of surprises and was proving to be the friendliest and most helpful country we had passed through so far. It was proving to be quite different from how I had imagined it to be.

"Breakfast at St. Goar"

ON WE GO

Dear Reader, you might wonder why we carried on, having had so many breakdowns but every time the fault had been fixed there was nothing more to dent our faith in the car's reliability. We thought that we had repaired everything that needed repairing. The radiator was now in better shape than ever it had been. What more could possibly go wrong?

On our way to the Ruhr District the weather became very hot. All the way along the journey we had found people to be so very friendly. In villages and towns people waved to us and smiled and truck drivers would give us a friendly toot as they overtook our car. They seemed to be able to travel much faster than we could, but we were in no hurry. At one point the road cut through a little hill, and we saw that ahead a man was watering his garden with a hosepipe. His garden was about two metres above the height of our road, behind a brick retaining wall. We waved to the man and we gestured to him and pointing at ourselves, inviting him to spray us with his hosepipe. Obligingly he swung the hose in our direction and gave us a very welcome, cooling, shower, thus demonstrating the benefits of an open topped car! Once while driving in the intense heat of the day I had to stop sharply. Droopy's brakes worked surprisingly well on this occasion, but the sudden halt and kinetic energy of the water had caused it to shoot skywards from out of the leaky radiator-cap. She blew off rather like a whale at sea. But water from a whale would be cold; water from the radiator was nigh on boiling. I suppose that instead, one should compare it to be more like a geothermal geyser, because of the scalding water. The radiator itself was now watertight though the cap itself was a poor fit. However, thankfully, throughout the rest of the trip we did not experience any more trouble from it.

The maps we had were not very informative. There were not many maps to be had in those days. The choice was very limited and the quality poor. Somehow we found our way through the industrialised Ruhr district via Neuss, and then through Duisburg and on to Bottrop. A few months previously my parents had entertained two German schoolteachers who had been over to England on a cultural exchange visit. They came to our house to experience a typically English Sunday roast lunch. The visit had been arranged through our village church. One guest had come from Bottrop and I had the idea that it would be a pleasant surprise for him, were we to drop by. How green, clean and pleasant the Ruhr and Bottrop were. It contrasted markedly with the grime of our industrial Black country at that time. In the evening we sat with our friend and a company of his friends at an open-air cafe in a beautiful park. In the background we could just see the top of a mineshaft's winding gear visible above the top of a row of beech trees. The people we met were charming, very polite and the whole atmosphere was very convivial and relaxed. Once again, Germany was not turning out at all as we had imagined or expected it might. One of the company we enjoyed spoke with a perfect English public-school accent. When I remarked upon it he said, "When I was a prisoner of war with the Americans they nicknamed me 'Limey'". Though he didn't get round to explaining how he acquired the accent.

We headed south, out and away from the Ruhr via Wuppertal and past Köln, which was written quite differently as: 'Cologne' on our English maps. We were learning fast as far as map reading was concerned. We found the River Rhein and followed it as far as Koblenz and once we were there we crossed over the river.

Often, as we drove down the side of the 'Rhine' (English version), we caught glimpses of a busy railway line running beside the road on our right, with the great river on our left. Both road and railway were very busy. Passengers on the passing trains and even some of the drivers of the flying express steam locomotives waved to us as they sped by, the latter sometimes giving us a hoot from their whistle. We were beginning to feel like royalty though there was no doubt that the car was the star. That night we camped at a large site near St. Goar. As usual Droopy attracted a considerable amount of interest and it was quite time consuming answering questions that people of a variety of nationalities posed, especially with their very limited English.

We had a fretful night's sleep being continually disturbed by noise. Traffic on the Rhein ran continuously all through the night. Noise from the loud chug-chug of the diesel engines and the many barges struggling against strong down-stream currents, the roar of passing trains and the motor traffic on the main road just outside the camp interrupted our sleep enormously. We were not in the best of moods the next morning. While we were trying to break camp, at the same time have some breakfast and then pack our things, more and more people came to look at Droopy Drawers to see and admire her. Several took photos often with us standing beside her. We thought we would never get away, but of course, in the end, we eventually did.

ROTATING TRAFFIC LIGHTS

I cannot remember when we first came across these strange traffic-lights on this trip. It might have been in the Ruhr but I am pretty sure we saw them in Mainz. We came up to a crossroads where I expected to see traffic-lights but there were none. We looked around and then spotted an object, which resembled a four-sided clock. It was suspended above by cables and positioned at the centre of the junction. We soon realised how they worked which one had to do pretty quickly, because if one hesitated the rest of the traffic would be hooting and hollering at you.

The face of this clock was divided into four equal sections or quadrants, two of which were painted green and the other two red. A hand on each clock face rotated slowly. When it pointed to green one could proceed and when one hand pointed to the red section one obviously had to stop. I thought they worked quite well and were easy to understand. However, they were phased out over the next few years but not before they controlled our progress through the maze that was Mainz.

There were no bypasses then.

The traffic lights. The 'clock' face was divided into four equal segments, two of them green and two red. The 'hand' at the centre rotated slowly, when it was on green you could precede; simple.

"Breaking New Ground"

DROOPY'S ROLE AS A PATHFINDER

We carried on up the Rhine valley. Just before Mainz we pulled into a petrol station to refuel. While we were there a 'GB' registered Morris Oxford pulled up behind us for a pit-stop. Bye and bye we got chatting with the occupants and compared notes.

"Did you go through Brussels?" they asked.

We told them that we had, and that we had a look around the city centre while we were there.

"Didn't you get lost?" they enquired.

"Er, no. Why?"

"Well we got hopelessly lost. Everyone does who tries to go through Brussels", they said. "It has a terrible reputation", and they added, "But you claim that you didn't, I find that hard to believe?"

"Well, no, not really. We didn't seem to experience any navigation problems".

"You mean to say you drove right through Brussels without getting lost AND you didn't have a problem?" To them that sounded incredible.

"Well, yes. No problem at all".

"That is amazing". They said in unison. Then their eyes lit up.

"Are we right to assume that you are going through Mainz today?" They asked earnestly.

"Well yes, we will probably carry on up the Rhine so I suppose we will". I replied.

"With your amazing navigational skills, could you act as our guide and could we follow you, please?" one of them asked.

We did not think we had any particular navigational skills but if they wanted to follow us, well that was up to them. We pointed out that we had never been to Mainz before and their guess was just as likely to be as good as ours, but they insisted that they wanted to follow us.

"Be it on your own heads, then, but I warn you it will be a case of the blind leading the blind". I said.

We went back to our respective vehicles. We had parked behind our new acquaintances and as I started up Droopy I said to Mike, "This, is going to be embarrassing".

So we pulled out in front of them in order to lead the way. I knew that Droopy was no match for a new Morris Oxford so I drove fast and rather recklessly so that I could at least try and generate and intensify the sporty image that (I liked to think) Droopy was supposed to exude. With only a seven-horse power side-valve engine and a three-speed gearbox, Droopy was not as sporty as she appeared to be at first glance. In the meantime Mike was trying his best to navigate but in my erratic haste I missed a crucial turning or two and found myself heading down a variety of narrow side streets. I looked in the mirror, quite thinking that Mr. Morris Oxford would have had the sense to give up following us and might have taken the correct turning, but no. There he was still on our tail and following closely as if in fear of losing us. I suppose sensibly, I should have stopped and admitted that I was, lost but I didn't out of pride and kept on going.

"Heh! Where the hell do you think you are going?" yelled Mike.

"I dunno, but I have this sixth sense that makes me think I am going in the right direction. Maybe if I dodge about we might pick up the main drag again."

"I might as well throw the bloody map away because I haven't got a clue where you are going."

Mike was getting quite agitated.

I turned towards him grinning and shouted, "Do you know Mike, neither have I."

Actually in busy urban streets even an Austin 7, driven hard and erratically, can provide quite a number of white-knuckle experiences. This ride had developed into all of that: with a few screechings of tyres, swerving and bumping over cobbles and negotiating tramlines and with the Morris Oxford hard on our heels. This scenario had all the ingredients of a car-chase. All that was lacking were the flashing blue lights of a German police car with the two-tone siren of De-Da, De-Da. British police cars still used bells, and adopted the siren latter.

Eventually this hair-raising drive through a maze of minor streets surprisingly brought us out onto a main road and even more surprisingly it turned out to be the right road to Worms. Somehow or other we couldn't tell anybody 'how', we were through and out of Mainz unscathed.

After a short distance further on clear of the urban development, I waved on the Morris Oxford to go ahead. There was no point in them continuing to stay behind us when they could go much faster. The car passed us but at the next convenient lay-by the driver got out and flagged us down. We obliged and pulled up behind him.

"I say. That was amazing," he exclaimed. "How on earth did you do it? Come on, you must have been to Mainz before! We could never have found our way through Mainz without you."

He was full of praise and thanks and I assured him that it was our first time in Germany let alone in Mainz. He offered to buy us a beer. He also claimed that he was dumbfounded to learn that anyone could find their way through Brussels without getting lost. Since then, over the years it seems to me that I do have a sixth sense when it comes to finding my way. It may of course be that I am lucky. However, over the years I have been through Brussels many times before the by-pass was built and have always unfailingly got lost.

Anyway, the friendly people in the Morris Oxford drove off and with their faster speed they gradually left us far behind and were gone from our lives forever.

We pulled over into a lay-by to say cheerio to our
friends in the Morris Oxford.

"Mosqitoes and Gauloise"

We had left behind the more scenic part of the Rhine Valley and we were in the flatter, more open country, which lay around Worms. We found a suitable campsite by the river but, as we quickly realised, it had a downside. We were plagued by mosquitoes. During the afternoon we had a look round the town and visited the particularly beautiful cathedral. The town was crawling with American troops and they even came to the campsite. At a moment when we had raised the bonnet of Droopy, two American soldiers strolled up to take a closer look at her. She must have appeared to them as a peculiar sort of creature. Uninvited they stuck their noses under the bonnet and peered into the engine bay. They did not speak to us but only talked between themselves. We might as well not have been there. Then concentrating on Droopy's engine, one of them said in a loud voice and with a large cigar in his mouth, mockingly, "Gee! Only four cylinders." I was a bit miffed by this and I replied, "Yes, and they have been going since before you were even thought of." They completely ignored me and swaggered off with their hands in their pockets and their noses in the air. "Good riddance to you." I said behind their retreating backs.

Later we were both lying in the sun on our groundsheet enjoying a rest and a drink of pop when a couple arrived in a small car. Despite bags of room on the site they decided to pitch their tent just in front of ours between us and the river. The girl was a very attractive blond, she settled herself down on their ground-sheet and watched her boyfriend busily set up their tent. The boy was fresh-faced and as a pair they could have passed for Hansel and Gretel from Grimm's Fairy Tales. He wore very short new Lederhosen and a white shirt and that appeared to be all. We noticed to our amazement that as he squatted down to hammer in shiny new metal tent-pegs using a new wooden mallet, he revealed most of his manly genitals hanging from the right side leg of his shorts. I was very embarrassed and looked at Mike who at that moment had taken a swig from his drink bottle. When he saw what I saw, he nearly exploded and spluttering rolled over onto his back like a puppy, struggling not to laugh out loud. It was a comical sight. Then he rolled back and resting on his elbows he managed, stifling his guffaws, to say, "What a pity we haven't got a catapult!"

Somehow we did not think it would be a good idea to warn 'Hansel'. 'Gretel' meanwhile, just lay there looking beautiful. She only had eyes for her boyfriend. She gazed longingly up at her industrious 'Hansel' with her admiring blue eyes as if she was spellbound. She surely must have noticed what was happening. Perhaps she was too shy to tell him and it was obvious that she had not drawn his attention to the show he was giving, as he continued to hammer in the pegs. Had he knelt down, instead of squatting, no-one would have noticed anything. 'Hansel' had provided us with a certain amount of free humourus entertainment.

In the late afternoon, and towards evening, mosquitoes came out in force. They became unbearable. Later we walked across the new bridge over the Rhine. There we found a small tobacconists and bought a packet of strong cigarettes. Once back at the tent Mike was persuaded to smoke the Galoise (as I did not smoke) and to fill the tent with the acrid stench of cigarette smoke. This proved to be quite effective at keeping the mozzies at bay. We were faced with the choice of choking to death or being eaten alive. We chose the former and the improvised insect repellent was very effective but at the same time it also acted as a human repellent. I had to burst out of the tent in desperation gasping for air several times throughout the night. By the time early morning arrived we were itching to get away! What happened to Hansel and Gretel how did he cope with the hungry mosquitoes? It makes one inclined to wince to even think about it.

We were itching to get away.
(Note the vents on the side of engine compartment utilising brass drawer-pulls).

"Broken Off"

STOPPING FOR A LEAK
Breakdown No. 6

For some reason or other Mike had an urge to return to France after we left Worms, so to pacify him, instead of going into Karlsruhe, I turned the car westwards and then south across the border and over the Rhine into France. We then decided to head directly for Strasbourg. We toodled steadily along without a care in the world until, after a while, Mike kept complaining that he could smell petrol, and the smell was strong. Actually had I been honest, I would have admitted that I could smell it too even in the driver's seat, but I did not like to admit it. I did not think it was very serious. However, eventually Mike begged me to stop, because he said, if I did not he would be sick. So reluctantly I pulled over and brought the car to a halt on a rough and ready roadside lay-by. While Mike was staggering around taking in large gulps of fresh air I decided that perhaps I should take a look under the bonnet to try and see if I could ascertain what was going on. That wasn't difficult! When I did, I found that the engine-bay simply reeked of petrol and the bulkhead at the back of the dashboard was wet, soaked with highly volatile fuel! Obviously something was radically wrong and I had to quickly figure out what it was, and what to do about it.

With Mike feeling a little better, I got him to start up and run the engine while I leaned over the engine compartment to try and see what the trouble was. Once the engine was running, it immediately became blatantly obvious as to where the leak was and what was causing the petrol to run out. An electrically driven pump was mounted on the engine-bay's rear bulkhead and from it a small-bore copper pipe carried fuel from the pump to feed the carburetor. That pipe had broken away from the union that connected it to the carburetor's inlet port. Petrol under slight pressure was squirting out uncontrollably and the draught generated by the cooling fan coupled with the wind from forward motion of the car had caused the petrol to spray back onto the bulkhead. The pump was mounted on the passenger side of the car and poor Mike was sitting directly behind it. No wonder he had felt sick. Amazingly some of the petrol was still finding its way into the carburetor, seemingly enough to have been sufficient to keep the engine going. That was a miracle in itself, but the major miracle was that she had not burst into flames and we hadn't been engulfed in a great ball of fire.

It was impossible for me to mend the pipe there and then at the roadside. This time there was no motor scooter man hanging around in the background waiting to come to our assistance and help us out of our predicament. We kept the bonnet open so that the petrol could evaporate in the hot sunshine. I decided to do a very temporary repair using insulating tape, and then we drove gingerly on until we came upon a small garage. We pulled in and I went into the workshop and found the proprietor, come mechanic. I detached the pipe and showed it to him and tried to explain the problem. Without so much as a word, no smile, no nothing; he just took the fuel pipe from me and he strode purposefully off into his workshop carrying the pipe delicately between his forefinger and thumb. I followed him and watched whilst he made a very neat job of repairing it, soldering it back together again. Having admired his own work, he passed the pipe to me, without so much as a word or a smile. It did not take me long to refit the pipe and connect it up. We were back in business. At his petrol pump I filled up with as much fuel as Droopy could take (we must have lost quite a lot through the leak en route). Although I paid for the petrol, the proprietor declined any offer of money for repairing the pipe.

And we were on our way once more, as far as I can remember without ever exchanging a single word with the garage proprietor. A case, surely, of actions speaking louder than words.

I assumed that the pipe had broken off because the carburetor had been mounted on the engine block and the pump on the bulkhead. They had been vibrating at different rates. Ideally there should have been a loop or sprung coil in the pipe run, or a flexible rubber section of pipe to absorb such movement between the various working parts, but sadly there wasn't.

Until then Droopy had remained true to form by never letting a day go by without providing us with some form of breakdown to test our patience. By then, she must have exhausted all possible variations of breakdown that she could dream up. From then on everything should surely proceed perfectly smoothly, and why shouldn't it?

We were very hungry by the time we arrived in Strasbourg. After we pitched the tent the evening was upon us. So we decided to live it up and go and have a meal in the town. This was to be our first proper meal out and we were somewhat apprehensive at the possible expense involved. We were not sure whether we had enough Francs to afford such a luxury. We needed to play it carefully. We set off with not a little trepidation.

Driving along the Rhine valley we would get a friendly wave or a hoot from passing locomotives

"Breaking a Record"

THE RESTAURANT

After wandering around Strasbourg doing a bit of sight-seeing, visiting the beautiful cathedral, and seeing all the storks nesting high up in trees in almost the center of town, we chose a nice tidy looking restaurant and entered rather nervously. Dining out was a new experience for both of us and being in a foreign country added to our anxieties. A waitress showed us to our table and gave each of us a menu. Mike told me to do the ordering, arguing that my French was better than his (which did not say much for his French). I felt that was a trifle unfair, as it was Mike who had wanted to return to France in the first place!

I studied the menu and tried to get a balance between the price and my understanding of what was on offer. I suggested chicken.

"Chicken. Is that expensive?" queried Mike.

"No. It is not the cheapest thing on the menu, but I know the French word for 'chicken'", I replied. Mike seemed to be happy with that, so when the waitress came to our table chicken was what we ordered, or so I had thought. She then asked if we wanted certain other things and as I did not understand I nodded my head said "Oui" a few times and added a few "S'il vous plaits" for good measure and asked for "deux biere".

The biere arrived fairly quickly accompanied by a plate of thin toast and pâté and some nicely presented salad. Mike gave me a quizzical look.

"Is this it?" he asked

"It's alright. Don't worry. I think it is all right, I think this is just the starters." I tried to reassure him, even though, to be honest, I wasn't absolutely sure.

At the next table there sat two very attractive girls who did not seem to be eating anything though they did have a glass of coloured soft drink in their hands. They sat there chatting away and giggling and kept looking in our direction, too often for comfort. This only added to the feeling of discomfort and embarrassment being in such unfamiliar surroundings. They, les girls, were still without any food. I remember one in particular, as she wore a thin white blouse, through which one could clearly see her white brassiere. One couldn't help noticing, though I didn't mention it to Mike. There was a long interval before our empty plates were cleared away. We were still very hungry. However this was quickly followed by the arrival of two steaming plates of soup in which were floating a few small dumplings. These were accompanied by a basket of bread.

Mike looked at me with a puzzled frown. "I thought you had ordered chicken?" he said. "Well honestly Mike, I'm sorry but honestly thought I had. Perhaps it is a kind of chicken soup? I suppose in a posh restaurant you cannot expect too much for your money." I added, "This is a touristy area, after all. If you are not happy you can jolly well do the ordering next time, but in the meantime we had better get our money's worth and make the most of this soup by eating it all up if this is all we're going to get."

Well satisfied, we sat for a while feeling rather bloated and eventually the waitress with whom we exchanged smiles removed our empty bowls.

"Is there a dessert of any kind, Ted?" asked Mike.

"Well to be perfectly honest, I'm not sure." I replied. "I think there might be but we had better wait a while, just to see. I can only pray though that if there is, it is not going to be very substantial because I am already more than well satisfied, and what really amounts to being absolutely and thoroughly stuffed and full to bursting."

"You ought to know jolly well what you ordered," mocked the now, highly irritated Mike. Then he stopped short. "Hey, hang on, it looks as if something more is coming our way."

With that announcement the next course arrived. I am sure we had a most puzzled look on our faces for two plates of a generous diameter were put in front of us, each one with a large domed stainless steel cover on it. Somehow, if only judging by the size, they did not look as if they would cover a dessert. We waited and then a third, even larger plate arrived also with a large silver looking dome with a handle on the top. We could not understand what was going on. We had thought we were finished. A waitress stood behind each of us, and then rather ceremoniously removed the stainless steel covers with a flourish to reveal a complete half-a-roast-chicken on each plate. Then off came the third cover showing various food items, which comprised mainly of vegetables.

Mike was horror struck. In fact we both were, our mouths open wide in astonishment and our eyeballs almost bursting from their sockets. We sat there in silence for what seemed to be an age, elbows resting on the edge of the table and fingers toying with the cutlery staring down at the feast before us.

The girls looked on eagerly, finding considerable amusement from our predicament.

"There you are," I cried triumphantly stabbing my fork in his direction and looking hard at Mike and I continued in some sort of irrational excitement, "You should not have doubted me. No. Look here's the chicken. I told you I ordered chicken, now didn't I?" I was rather proud that I had actually got the order right even with the handicap of my limited French.

"But you did not know for certain, now did you? Come on, own up and be honest just for once." Said Mike sarcastically.

Mike paused for a moment or two. Then he continued, "But I tell you, I cannot eat that. I cannot possibly eat another blinking thing. I am full up to my ears as it is. You should have warned me to go easy on the starters if you really knew there was chicken coming, ah ha, but you didn't now did you?"

Mike was working himself up into a state especially as another large dish with more vegetables arrived. I glanced furtively around; the girls were still looking at us. "Curse". "Gordon Bennett, what are we going to do? We should not have eaten so much of the dumplings and that rotten soup. That was filling enough by itself. I tell you, I'm full up to the ears. "We cannot very well not eat it. We've got to make an effort and try. Think of England."

We did our best, but it was a huge struggle even to make the slightest impression on so much food. We could not understand how the French could eat so much at one sitting but being British we felt we could not let our Queen and country down, so we persevered as best we could, feeling that we now had some idea of what it must be like to be a force-fed goose.

"Now I know what those geese must feel like, I said to Mike, blowing through my teeth.

"How very, very cruel that is. I feel I have just broken a record on the amount of food I have eaten at any one time."

As if all that had not been enough there was a dessert to follow. A desert! We paid the hefty bill and staggered out onto the street, feeling fit to burst and extremely uncomfortable. The two French girls had continued still giggling and chatting away, sipping their drinks slowly. They smiled at us and watched our every move. I rather think we missed an opportunity there. We should have invited them to our table. At the very least they would have helped us consume some of the food, thereby doing us a favour. Romance however, was not on the menu after that meal! No way!

Out on the street we wandered slowly around with no special place in mind. We could hardly move so we had to force ourselves to walk, desperately trying to burn off calories. In the early hours of the morning we found our way back to our car, and drove to the campsite. Our intention was to be as quiet as possible so as not to disturb other sleepers and give us British a bad name.

As we swung into the campsite we nearly ran over some campers sleeping on the grass. It was such a hot night they had not bothered to even erect their tent so they were sleeping out in the open. Not long after we had bedded down, another party arrived even later than us. Later or early which ever way one wants to look at it. They disturbed the whole camp with their noise, shouting and laughing without any concern for others who might be asleep. Regrettably, we realised they were English speaking. At least they had deflected any criticism that may have been directed at us for returning late. These days, most camping and caravan sites are managed more strictly and shut their gates at 20.00 hours. Which is much better.

We slunk away from the site fairly late in the morning and decided to head back into Germany across a bridge over the Rhine and on to Freiburg. There we made a brief walking tour round the town to view some of the sites and then returned to the market square. When we returned to the place where we had parked the car, we heard a distant sound, slightly muffled, like Droopy's horn, but there appeared to be no sign of Droopy. Where we thought we had parked her, a rather large and excited crowd had gathered. Then from the middle of that crowd came the familiar sound: 'Barrp, barrp' again. It dawned on us that this crowd was surrounding Droopy and hiding her from us. As we eased our way through to the car, people seemed very pleased to see us. Everyone was very good-natured and when I got into the driving seat and gave them a rendering of the klaxon's best sounds, which they had not heard before, it sent them into gales of laughter, cheering and clapping. I started her up and tickled the throttle a few times to give the onlookers a rendering of her un-silenced throaty exhaust: 'Verrooom, bang, Err-err', which delighted our audience even more. Our departure was delayed for a quite a while longer when we found that several people with cameras wanted a photo or two, and so we posed sitting in and standing beside the car. We then finally left them; it was quite a send off, amid cheers applause and very friendly waving. It was a thrill to be a celebrity for a moment, however fleeting. We were definitely back in the friendliest country we had experienced on our continental journey so far.

When we returned to our car we couldn't see it, only a large crowd, but we soon began to hear it!

"Breakaway"

BADEN-BADEN
Breakdown No. 7

We were on the B500 and were just entering the magnificent town of Baden-Baden, en route to the Black Forest. As usual I was engaging in what I thought was a deft display of nifty double-de-clutch gear-changing when, just at the critical moment in the middle of a complex and busy traffic junction, the gear-lever came away in my hand. Just like that! Rather horrified and worried, I managed to keep the car going even though it was stuck in the second of the three gears. I was desperately looking for a place to stop and all the time clutching the unattached lever in my left hand. The town was very busy, clogged with expensive cars. It was essential for us to stop, so that we could examine and sort out the gear-lever situation. The gearlever would need to be re-attached somehow before we went much further. One cannot drive very far without being able to change gear!

Everywhere we went on this trip was a new experience for us. We had no idea what sort of a town Baden-Baden was. However it did not take many minutes before we realised that it was a bustling but rather exclusive place; very opulent, rather elegant, posh and prestigious. The likes of which we humble souls had never cast our eyes upon before. It appeared to be full of wealth and luxury. Finely clad people walked the pavements, their clothes fashionable and embellished with items of jewelry and furs. They looked 'terminally rich' as if they could never possibly have experienced financial hardship. Women of all ages paraded their finery and appeared as if they could never at any time in their lives have a care in the world.

We crawled past the magnificent Casino Building and Kurhaus with their lovely grounds, still nursing Droopy along, stuck in her second gear. We also passed the beautiful Opera House and the very Grand Theatre but still could not find a place to stop. Had there been a parking place available anywhere I would probably have been too embarrassed to come to a halt in such grand surroundings. I should perhaps mention here, that since the days of our little tour the town's traffic layout has changed dramatically and the main National Route 500 now bypasses the town completely by going underground through a long tunnel.

We felt very much out of place in Baden-Baden and we would have rather stood out amongst the well dressed, cigar smoking, ivory cigarette-holders, homburg and astrakhan hat-wearing inhabitants and tourists, with Toy-boys, and toy-dogs, etc. Even though I had spotted a free parking place by the Casino, we were not tempted to go in for a flutter, so I decided to pass on. I just could not bring myself to try to mend the gear lever whilst among the huge limousines with their sleek chauffeurs, the Rollers, Mercedes and the Porches. It would have shown Droopy up for the mongrel she was.

So I nursed Droopy on until we were out of the town and eventually rolled into a suitable lay-by. Affecting this particular repair was fortunately comparatively easy for a change. A small diameter precision-machined stainless-steel pin, which held the gear lever in place, had worked its way out possibly due to the vibrations, which had caused so much havoc with other parts of the car. It had dropped onto the car's floor. Very luckily despite its small size we managed to find it trapped in a small crevice by the handbrake mechanism. It could have so easily dropped through any of the several holes in the floor and fallen down onto the road, where we would never have found it. As one would have expected under 'Sod's-Law', our Guardian Angel was looking after us again. Once I had extricated the 3cm long pin from the small crevice, I quickly relocated the gearlever in its proper position then forced the retaining pin back into place. It was a 'force-fit' and I tapped it in comparatively easily with a large spanner used as an improvised hammer. Once I had made sure the pin was a tight fit, we were back in business.

Surely that must mean that we now had seen the back of breakdowns. That last one must have been the very, very last of our problems. What else was there left that could possibly go wrong? That surely had to be the last of the gremlins that Droopy could have had hiding up her sleeve. Comforted by that logic we decided to press on with our journey. And why not?

"It just came away in my hand".

"A Break in the Clouds"

THE BLACK FOREST TRAIL
Die Schwarzwald-Hochstrasse

After Baden-Baden we headed in a southerly direction climbing steadily to and through the Black Forest via Lake Titisee, then Donaueschingen and Stockach until we came to Lake Constance (Bodensee) and then proceeded along its northern shoreline to the resort of Überlingen. Due to a very winding road rich in sharp bends twisting and climbing up to 850metres, our journey had been rather torturous and consequently arduous for driver and car. We had taken it rather gently nursing Droopy slowly up and around the curves until we made it safely to the summit. Good old Droopy she showed she could do it much to our relief, but then we were up, that was only part of the story. Eventually we had to come down and I was always conscious that we had ineffective brakes. What goes up must come down. I had to rely heavily on the gears to slow us down. But we made it safely. Thank you Droopy!

The weather changed and took a turn for the worse. We arrived on the outskirts of Überlingen in heavy rain. This certainly was not camping weather so we opted instead to stay at a Gasthof which we came across called Gletschermuhle. This guesthouse was run by a pair of elderly and matronly sisters who looked after us very well. We were given a pleasant room overlooking the lake but it was a great pity that the rain spoiled our view.

This may seem strange now in the 21st century to admit that it was our first experience of sleeping under a duvet. In 1957 they were unheard of in England. It was another 20 years before they started to be commonly used in the UK. The view across the lake had improved by morning. The clouds had rolled away and we could see across to the opposite shore. We threw off the duvets and Mike, hypnotized by the view across the lake with the sight of the magnificent Alps in the background, began to pour over the road atlas.

"That must be Switzerland we can see on the other side," he said.

"**We have to do Switzerland**." We both said simultaneously, looking at each other eagerly. So it was decided, there and then, that Switzerland was to be our next destination.

That morning we set off along the lake, back the way we had come with the idea of bearing off at the end of the lake and enter Switzerland via Basel which was further to the west. It had not occurred to us that there were ferries that could have taken us across the lake more directly and quicker.

It was raining again as we started off, as we left the guesthouse. A Volkswagen Beetle suddenly slid past us rotating as it went and carried on down the road going backwards. It missed us, but it had been a close shave.

"That's the snag with cars with rear engines," said Mike with authority. "Even if you simply brake you could end up in a skid. It is because they have all their weight at the back, where the engine is housed, and the heavy end, just like a dart, always wants to go first."

Droopy might have slid about a bit but she did not have that tendency despite all the luggage stacked on the back.

Negotiating the Black Forest proved a tough test for Droopy, but she coped well (if not slowly). At least the road surfaces were good.

"Breaking under the strain"

TROUBLE BREWING

The drive to Lake Titisee through the Black Forest and on down to Lorrach had been pretty arduous and required great concentration. It had been very hilly and we had negotiated many hairpin bends. I noticed with some anxiety that the car seemed to have developed another new problem. I had not said anything to Mike, but the fault appeared to be getting worse. Eventually I felt I had to tell him, that I thought the car was not running smoothly. I explained, that every time we went round a sharp left-hand bend the off-side rear wheel appeared to rub on the bodywork and the noise that it made was audible to me at least, even if he hadn't noticed it. Eventually we decided to stop and shift as much of the baggage as possible over to the left hand side of the car. The idea being that by moving the weight away from the problem it would reduce the rubbing. Well that may have eased the problem very slightly, but it certainly had not cured it completely.

The weather improved and I drove very gingerly on the last leg of the journey into Lorrach. I was worried indeed. If we were unable to identify the problem how could we determine what action might be necessary to attempt a repair, assuming that we would be able to. The big question was: "should we dare to venture any further with the rear wheel rubbing against the bodywork as it was?" There were signs of rubbing on the body underneath the rear mudguard. We could not afford to ignore the evidence. Problems like that do not usually disappear, they just get worse. In the end we decided to sleep on it until the next morning.

At breakfast we found that we had completely run out of methylated spirits for our stove. It was decided that I should drive into town to buy more on my own so the car had the least amount of load to carry and that I could also see how she behaved. Hoping against hope that the problem had indeed gone away overnight, I parked outside a Droguerie without any trouble and I went up the steps into the shop. I did not know the word for 'methylated' in German so I tried the word in English first. That drew a blank, so I tried the word in French, which I thought was: 'alcohol a bruler'. The female assistant brought a bottle of what appeared to be plain clear water or maybe it was just pure alcohol. I shook my head and said "Nein". The girl seemed taken aback and she consulted with her colleagues. Then the practitioner emerged from the back of the shop and entered into the debate with several customers. The outcome was, that the chemist confirmed, that the first bottle they had offered to me was what I was looking for by saying: "Ja, das ist es. Es is Spiritus oder alcohol a bruler, genau was Sie brauchen."

Everyone in the shop seemed to agree with him, some earnestly nodding their heads to each other and I began to get the gist of what he was saying. I came up with an idea to solve this impasse and confidently unscrewed the bottle top. I was convinced that it was not meths as, after all meths was a purple, and not clear like water. I took a sniff of the liquid with the concentrated gaze of all those gathered around me. I was the center of attention all right! Then I sniffed again. Hmm. It did smell a little bit like meths, but not perhaps so strong as the British stuff.

"Es ist für Camping, Nicht wahr?" said the chemist reassuringly. The word 'camping' was definitely a clue, so I gave in and purchased the bottle but I was not completely convinced, that I had got what I wanted. I said goodbye to everyone in the shop who had been so patient with me, so polite and so very helpful. I had caused a bit of a commotion, and left one behind me, that is for sure. In my ignorance I had not realised that British methylated spirits is in fact alcohol which has been dyed purple to deter alcoholics from drinking it. I left the shop and made my way back to the car carrying my purchase.

"Weak-end Break"

TRAPPED IN THE CAR PARK

I made my way out of the chemists down the steps and out to Droopy parked in front of the building. I jumped in and started her up and put her into reverse, for the moment I had forgotten about the rubbing wheel. Something rather weird happened. As the car reversed it felt strangely, as if it was going over an extraordinary large hump or stone. I leaned forward a bit to take a look over the side and at the off-side rear wheel. I could see nothing that was in the way on the ground that could have caused an obstruction. Puzzled I tried reversing again and the same thing occurred. Then I drove a foot or two forward and everything seemed as normal. This was very strange. It felt as if there was an invisible bump on the ground. I got out of the car and went to the rear. I could see nothing in the way to prevent the car from reversing. This was more puzzling still. There was no kerb or stone – nothing. I felt that Droopy was playing games with me, and I became extremely concerned. What the heck was going on?

I decided to get back in the car and to try to reverse again, but this time I would do so looking over the side and towards the rear off-side wheel to see if I could work out what could be wrong. I put Droopy into reverse and drove her very gently backwards. All the time watching to see what was happening, and I became absolutely thunder-struck at what I saw. As the car started to move backwards, the rear wheel itself, stayed exactly where it was. But the driver's seat became positioned over that wheel. It could not, and should not, be physically possible! I jumped out and got down on the ground so that I could see under the car. Inspecting the underside I saw to my horror, that the back-axle casing was broken close to the differential. It was completely broken and not just cracked. My stomach sank and it felt as if it was screwed up in knots. What a disaster! The amazing thing was, that despite the broken casing the half-shaft had not broken too. It became horribly and painfully clear now, why the off-side rear wheel had been rubbing against the bodywork the day before. This was a really serious turn of events and we were in an extremely unhappy predicament. What now?

To be able to drive out of the car park I needed to turn Droopy around. To achieve this manoeuvre, I pushed the car backwards by hand very gently and slowly. Then I jumped in and drove the Droopy forward a little. I repeated these manoeuvres, back and forth until I had turned the car sufficiently for me to drive forwards out of the car park in first gear. I drove gingerly back to the campsite all the way there wondering what on earth we were going to do.

"You have been a long time" complained Mike. "Did you get the meths?"

"I'm not sure if it is the right liquid but this is what I did get." I handed him the bottle.

"What's the Hell is this supposed to be?" He held up the bottle and looked at me quizzically and I should add, sternly.

I explained to him all about the bother I had experienced in the chemist's shop and suggested that we should give it a try. After all we had nothing else we could use.

"What's up?" asked Mike. He must have notice that I was looking rather worried. I then told him about the very serious problem with the car – just a mere broken back axle I explained!

He looked at me aghast. "You've got to be joking!" He almost shouted, stamping his feet in frustration.

"Take a look under the car for yourself." I said dismally. He looked sideways at me for a moment as he did, what I suggested. He got down and peered under the back of the car. He too was dumbstruck.

After a few moments and after letting out a whistle, he got up slowly up from the ground by the car and dusted off his hands.

"Phew, blimey! So now what?" he exclaimed.

"'Now what' indeed!" I replied.

"The Breaker's Yard"

THE MOTHER OF ALL BREAKDOWNS
Breakdown Number 8

The 'Alcohol-a-bruler seemed to work. It enabled us to conjure up a cup of tea over which we meditated and considered our predicament and tried to decide what to do next for the best.

Initially the only option I could think of, was to dump everything including the car and try to hitch-hike home with only our basic essentials. Obviously we would have to forget about going to Switzerland, that idea was now definitely struck off the menu. As we debated, the 'dumping everything' idea seemed to have some merit. Alternatively I could go out and see if I could find a garage, which carried out major car repairs. If there was the slightest chance, that Droopy could be repaired and restored to some sort of ravaged glory, it seemed to us, that this second idea could hardly be an option. It was so unlikely to be successful. However, in the end we decided to give the latter a go before giving up entirely. It might not be just a rather long shot, and rather expensive to boot. Assuming that we found such a garage, could they get hold of a new back axle? It was worth a try, because if the car could be mended, then how much easier it would be for us to get home!

So we decided to give it a go and we began searching for a suitable garage. I drove along with great care, because I had no alternative. One thing was certain and that was, we couldn't drive all the way home like this. Mike came with me, just in case I might need him to provide a bit of pushing power, if it became necessary to reverse – and also for a bit of moral support. The car seemed to be going along smoothly enough, providing we drove slowly and steadily. It wasn't a time for sharp cornering. Eventually we came to a garage. I drove gingerly into the forecourt and parked the car in such a way, that it would be possible to exit their forecourt without the need to reverse. I sought out a member of staff and started to explain our dilemma and asked about the possibility of a repair. Using that magical international word:- "Kaputt", coupled with some noises and sign language and at the same time pointing under the rear of our car. The men in the garage soon grasped the nature of our trouble. The man I took to be the service manager inspected the damaged axle, uttered some incomprehensible words and then with a gasp muttered "Mein Gott! Hmmm!" He gathered himself up off his feet then brushed his hands on his overalls. He faced us, scratching his head under his army field cap. Then he cleared his throat, pursed his lips and took a deep breath. He shook his head several times, whilst at the same time moving his hands from side to side across his chest and said emphatically, "Nein". Without further ado he turned on his heels and walked back into the workshop. He had washed his hands of us! Mike looked dejected and stood silently by. I did the same. Each of us was deep in our own thoughts, when a youngish man came up to us and coughed politely.

"Entschuldigen Sie bitte, darf ich Ihnen helfen?"

How could he possibly help us, I thought? He is just a young man on a scooter. However, what had we got to lose, even if I had to go through the process of explaining our trouble all over again, which was difficult with the limited German we shared between us. However, we did our best to explain our predicament. He thought and reflected for a while and then said, "Hmmm. Kommen Sie mit." He walked back to his scooter, pointed to Droopy and beckoned for us to follow him. He got on his scooter and waited for us by the road with his noisy 2-stroke engine idling. He kept looking round to see, if we were coming. We decided we had nothing to lose; any port in a storm so to speak. We had had positive results from young men on scooters before, so we headed out to the road and off we went after him; to where we knew not. "Yah, I wish he wasn't going so fast. He seems to forget that we've got a broken back-axle", I cried as I struggled in the urban traffic to keep him in sight and at the same time nursing Droopy-Drawers along as best I could. I felt that I could feel her pain. We followed him for several kilometres and were just wondering, if we should give up and stop. He was going at an impossible speed for us to be able to keep up with him.

"I pray that the half-shaft doesn't break. I fear that it will fail any minute. In fact I can't understand why it has not done so already." I said to Mike, anxiously gritting my teeth. "Do you think he is playing a joke on us?"

"I don't know what to think, but we can't keep chasing after him like this for much longer! Hang-on, he's just turning off right. Where in Hell's name is he leading us?" said Mike.

The man on the scooter had turned off the road along a rough track. We followed him gingerly. It was a track which lead to a huge......... We could not believe it. I am sure I turned pale.

"Look at all the wrecked cars! There's stacks of them. It's a blasted breaker's yard. " I cried out in horror. "Do you think this is his idea of a joke or something? Or do you think, he seriously thinks, that our car is a 'write-off' and that we need somewhere to dump it?" I was thinking out loud to myself. "Of course, he could be right we may have to do just that!"

We were certainly baffled and bewildered. We came to a stop in the middle of the scrap yard surrounded by a mountainous pile of rusty and battered cars, bits of plant machinery, large, odd metal pieces and plate. We bumped along after him, until he came to a halt in the yard. We could see the scooter, that we had been following, parked on its stand outside some large corrugated iron and rather dilapidated sheds. Its rider had disappeared into one of the sheds but after a while he emerged followed more slowly by two workmen in overalls. One of them, to put it mildly, was rather obese. He wore greasy, green, ragged and patched rather grubby overalls and a battered Tyrolean trilby hat, which may well have started off in life grey in colour. My goodness, he had quite a gut on him, and could well have passed for being nine months pregnant. Another slightly slimmer man wore a grubby, navy blue workshop fitter's jacket, grubby and patched grey trousers and what had probably been a German Army Government surplus field-cap. In those days Field-caps seemed to be very popular or so we had noticed. He was a stocky tough looking character and to my eyes, they both had a rather unsavoury appearance. I was worried.

They approached us, rubbed their hands on their filthy clothing and then held them out and shook our hands very amicably.

"Oh ho! So Eure Achse ist gebrochen- hmmm" the fat one said. Their faces were beaming, as if they found our trouble highly amusing.

What followed from then on was, that we communicated with a lot of sign-language. The one we assumed to be the boss indicated, that we should start up the car. By miming with his hand and grasping an imaginary steering wheel he indicated with a turn of his head and pointing, that we should drive down a track stacked high on either side with car body shells and skeletons of scrapped vehicles.

I thought, "That's it, we are heading for the crusher". We took the direction indicated, which in a short distance brought us up in front of a large open-fronted shed. The Boss caught up with us, rather short of breath and indicated, that I should drive over a service pit that was in the center of the building. The pit seemed a bit wide for our narrow wheel-based car. I was anxious, but showing off as usual and not wanting to let the side down, I tried to exhibit my driving skills and confidently drove over the pit. There was a loud shout from the Boss. Something wasn't right.

"Ach. Nein" He held his hands over his eyes. His face bore a look of horror.

I could not imagine, why he was startled and worried, so I jumped out of the car to take a look. I could see immediately, why he was so rattled. Two of Droopy's wheels were perched on top of the kick-plate that surrounded the lip of the pit. I got back into the driver's seat and was gently pushed by the workmen a few feet back from off the pit. It was so scary – I could easily have fallen into the pit with Droopy! That would not have been funny. At my second attempt to drive over and straddle the pit, I paid very careful attention to the fellows guiding me. Precision was of the essence. The pit was of course designed for larger and more modern vehicles with a wider wheelbase. Droopy only just fitted over the pit and straddled its kick-plates.

It became obvious that they intended to perform some sort of miracle on poor Droopy's broken transmission. Quite what, was a question. But, whatever, it represented a stay of execution. For the moment she was not going to be fed into the crusher's hungry jaws. We crossed our fingers. What I did not understand at the time, was why only the back-axle seemed to go out of line, when the car was driven in reverse. Perhaps I would find out.

The Boss got to work with his helper. He called (yelled) out in a loud guttural voice.

"Heinrich, Heinie, hier mal!"

A fresh-faced young man, also wearing overalls, emerged from the interior of one of the tumbledown sheds, that we had seen upon entering the yard. He was blinking from being exposed to the bright sunshine but came briskly over, to where we were standing. We were introduced to Heinrich, we shook hands and the Boss then told him what was required of him. Heinrich went promptly into the pit to inspect and assess the damage under the car, while the Boss and his buddy settled down on two old and battered dining chairs. As we stood by feeling uncomfortable and not knowing quite what to do, the seated men muttered between themselves. We waited nervously to see, what the diagnosis would be.

"Heinrich!" the Boss bellowed. Heinrich's head emerged from under the car.

"Heinrich, hole mal eine paar Stühle."

Heinrich obediently trotted off to disappear among the conglomeration of ramshackle buildings. In those days our knowledge of German was lamentably limited, so we had no idea what was being said. It soon became apparent, what Heinrich had gone to fetch. He re-appeared with a chair under each arm, set them down and made a little bow towards us. The Boss also gestured that the chairs were for us. Heinrich headed off to one of the other sheds but was stopped midway by a shout from the Boss.

"Heinrich." he yelled, "Bier, Heinrich, bier!" Heinrich peeled off in a different direction followed by another roared order.

"Und ein Öffner– ein Öffner" Heinrich raised an arm in acknowledgement and without looking round disappeared.

The boss looked at us, smiled and nodded reassuringly. After another few minutes Heinrich reappeared, half shuffling, half trotting, carrying two crates of beer for us. He edged his way along beside the car and lowered the crates beside the Boss who leant from his chair to pull out one bottle at a time for distribution. He took the bottle opener (Öffner) from poor, sweating, Heinrich's outstretched hand and indicated that it should be passed on to Mike. Then it was my turn. I also received one, again via Heinrich who gave it to me with his very polite bow. The Boss then gave one to his mate and then lastly took one for himself. He held up his beer and offered us a toast.

"Zum Wohl – Prosit." He bellowed, followed by a gurgling chuckle and his body shook gently in mirth.

"Danke schön – Cheers." We politely returned the toast.

Heinrich hesitated but with a nod from his boss he turned on his heel heading back again to one of the ramshackle sheds. "Poor Heinrich is doing all the work and didn't get a drink." I whispered to Mike.

"Prosit." Bellowed the Boss again as he raised his bottle, then emptying it in one long gulp. The empty bottle went straight into the crate and in one continuous movement out came another beer. The Boss nodded to us, grinned held up his bottle and took another large swig, savoured it, swallowed and let out belches of satisfaction. His helpmate, who was taking his drink more slowly, held up his bottle to us in a toast of friendship too. It struck us, as being a very jolly and convivial atmosphere.

We then saw poor Heinrich, he was always the one doing all the work. He arrived with a heavy electrical arc-welding transformer trolley, complete with a mask and welding rods, which he assembled. He then collected his tools and went down into the pit and began to get to work on Droopy's back-axle. We could not help feeling sorry for the lad, but the Boss and his mate did not show the slightest degree of compassion for him. They were in a very jolly mood and now on their third beer, while Mike and I were still on our first. They showed a great capacity for drinking and the Boss getting jollier by the minute produced a large cigar, prepared it with his buddy's Swiss-army knife and then produced a lighter.

In the meantime from down in the pit, there came grinding and banging noises, plus some energetic hammering. Sparks and spitting from grinding and arc welding flew up through the smoke issuing out of the pit.

This was accompanied by a certain amount of cursing and the smell from overheated engine oil. As the repair activity was going on, the Boss drew deeply on his cigar, emitting large puffs of bluish smoke. He then staggered to his feet, raised his right hand in which was his cigar and made a 'V' sign and in a low octave voice growled, "Vin-ston Chur-chill. Who-ha, ha-haha. Who-haha."

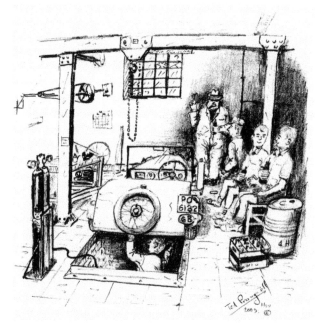

Then he sat heavily down onto his chair and rolled about slapping his knees and laughing. His body shook as he enjoyed his own joke. We joined in with the best sympathetic laughter we could muster. However we began to find the situation so hilarious that we too burst out laughing uncontrollably. A very jolly time was being had by all bar poor Heinrich who was still beavering away under the car, sweating his guts out down in the dark, dirty and sweltering pit.

Eventually Heinrich appeared from under the car, hot, red faced and sweating profusely. He gathered up all his equipment and then stood hands on hips, studied the car for a few moments, turned towards us to give us a tilting nod of his head and a thumbs-up. He then unexpectedly broke into a smile; a smile of confidence that he had fixed the problem and it was a job well done. In my eyes he had achieved the impossible! While he stood there, I walked round to the crate, picked out a bottle of beer, looked at the Boss and held out the bottle enquiringly towards Heinrich.

"Oh, ja, ja, natürlich, natürlich. Ja, sicher, sicher." said the Boss. He rocked back and forth on his chair and raised his hand confirming his agreement.

Poor Heinrich must have been gasping with thirst. He received his well-earned beer with a little bow and was obviously very appreciative. The Boss stuffed his cigar in his mouth as he stood up, followed by his buddy, and he motioned to us with his hands, a pushing movement. With his palms facing forward indicating, that we should get Droopy off the pit and out of the shed. So I clambered into the driver's seat, started her engine, gingerly reversed out of the shed and then turned the car around ready to leave. It felt wonderful especially as the back wheel didn't hump up like it had been doing before the welding.

What a relief!

I did my best to ask, how much it cost for the repairs but the Boss just gestured with open hands waving us away then shrugged his shoulders. He straightened himself up as best he could, raised his hand with his cigar, made another 'V' sign, and did his "Vin-ston Chur-chill; Ha ha ha" performance once again. Full of laughter and smiles, he shook our hands, gave us a friendly nod, a thump on the shoulder and shushed us away.

"Ach! Geht weg, geht weg. Gute Reise Jungens, kommt gut nach Haus, eh?" We shook hands all round and tried to show emphatic appreciation of their kindness. They were standing in a little group, when we left the yard. We were rather sad to leave them.

We did not really know where we were, but we managed to retrace our route to the campsite, as between us we were able to remember one or two landmarks that we had passed on the way to the scrap yard. We were lost in our own thoughts after our amazing experience. Suddenly something occurred to me.

"I say Mike, whatever happened to the chap on the scooter," I asked. "Where did he vanish to?"

"I've no idea, Ted. Like you, I did not notice him leave but where would we have been without him? That's the second time a scooter rider has helped us. Another Guardian Angel, and that's for sure".

"Brakeless"

HOMEWARD BOUND

When we got back to the tent we held a 'council of war'. We had to decide what our next move should be. Switzerland was tempting and beckoned us seductively from just down the road or from across the lake. But after so many breakdowns it would have been tempting providence to venture any further away from home. The prudent thing would be for us to head for Calais. We had plenty of time to get there and catch our ferry, but only if we had no more serious breakdowns.

"Why can't we Mike? Whatever else could possibly go wrong?" I reasoned with Mike. "We have fixed everything that needed fixing, so I repeat: what else could go wrong?" I had posed that question before, earlier on our trip, I remembered. Were they my famous last words?

"I suppose" said Mike "we cannot be sure, if the back-axle will hold together. Remember that we have already experienced French roads, and found them to be the worst we have ever encountered." Mike reasoned and of course he was right.

So we agreed, that it would be irresponsible and foolhardy to continue our journey any further away from home. Next morning we would strike camp and sensibly head back for Calais. We faced a long drive ahead of us.

We packed up and left Lorrach the next morning, bound for home. We headed north and crossed the Rhine at the first available bridge over the river. This was at the town of Breisach about 12 km due west of Freiburg. The bridge, a narrow combined road and rail bridge, had a wooden deck. It was a steel-framed Warren-girder type of bridge that had been erected by the allied forces during or shortly after WW2. Droopy had fairly narrow tyres and I had to be careful not to get the wheels trapped in the rails. I straddled one side of the track as I drove across the bridge. I was worried what would happen, if we met a vehicle coming in the opposite direction, or worse than that a train! I had not seen any railway signals or traffic lights that could have given us any warning. Thankfully we met neither train nor another motor vehicle and the crossing was completed successfully.

Then we were back in France and approached the customs post, which involved the usual business of exchanging the Triptyque documents. That business over with and done, we were off again. We passed through Colmar and approached the Vosges Mountains. I remember the road had a good surface and whilst it was a long climb the gradients were not too severe. We took it very gently and crawled slowly and steadily up in bottom gear. It was only slightly quicker than walking! Droopy was on her best behaviour and did not even boil. The axle was fine and soon we were going over the Col-du-bon-homme which was reputed to be 1220metres high. After that it was mostly all downhill. We were beginning to regret curtailing our tour and heading home.

I cannot remember exactly when it was, but I do remember, that we were going reasonably fast (fast for Droopy) when we approached a fairly sharp bend. I pushed my foot hard on the brake pedal to slow down the car, but it had no effect. I saw that there was a tiny minor farm road that veered off to the right and which rose up as a slight incline. I made a split-second decision and swerved sharply off the highway to drive up the side-road to rely on the incline to bring the car to a stop.

"Hey," Mike shouted. "What an earth are you doing? Where do you think you are going?"

Now with things under control, and I had actually come to a stop, I explained to Mike what was amiss. He was looking pretty worried and was wondering, whether the brakes had deteriorated so badly that they were no longer working at all. I was thinking that also. I got out of the car and tweaked the cables a bit in case they had stretched, as they were inclined to do. I then tested them and was able to demonstrate to Mike that they were now working sufficiently well to lock the offside rear wheel. I promised to be more careful for the rest of the run down that descent. I must admit that I had had a bit of a fright too, but I had kept that quiet.

For a while the journey was generally uneventful. We had descended the Vosges through Gerardmer then we drove through Epinal, Neufchateau, Rheims and Laon. The car was managing really well or so I had thought, until Droopy seemed to be getting into a truculent mood and her steering appeared to be wandering. Was it my driving? Was I imagining it? Perhaps she was sulking and did not want to go home! Then the steering got worse. I began to wonder, whether it was the back axle playing up again. Driving her was getting really scary as she was wandering about even on the straightest of roads. It was no use, I had to stop and check her over, before we had a collision with somebody or some object or other.

"Breaking Apart"

FLOATING FRONT AXLE
Breakdown No. 9

This time it wasn't the back axle. We established that upon examination. The back axle was perfectly sound and the welded repair was holding up well. Which was great news, but it didn't solve the current problem.

This time there was something wrong with the steering. When we eventually realised where the fault lay, it was not good news. Not at all!

Droopy was fitted with a pair of radius arms. These took the form of a pair of 1¼" x 1¼" steel angle pieces which spread out in a 'V' formation to act as a brace. The point of the 'V' was fixed to the engine bay's bulkhead. These struts were splayed out forward to the front axle to which they were attached. They acted as braces to keep the configuration of the front axle true and to hold it steady. The brace or strut on the left side had broken in two at the mid point along its length, which meant, that the front axle was no longer rigid and because of that, it was moving about. This had affected the steering, and not surprisingly it was causing the car to wander.

What should we do? We could not precede any further in safety, as one of the fundamentals of driving a car was to be able to steer it and aim it in the right direction. There was not a house in sight from where we might have sought assistance, and the only building we could see was a nearby dilapidated shed or small barn, which was standing in a field not far from the roadside. I came up with the idea, that if we could possibly find a straight solid piece of wood, I could affect a temporary repair using the wood as a splint. The wood needed to be straight and strong and of a suitable length. We foraged around and hunted in the shed. Each of us returned to the car with a selection of pieces of wood, that we had found, in the hope, that one of them would be the right thickness, strength and length. We did not have a saw, but I did have a hacksaw blade in my tool kit that came in useful. We settled on a straight, roughly 2"x2" rectangular section of timber, that we had salvaged from the shed. I needed some wire to be able to fix it in place. So I then clambered down the bank at the side of the road, jumped across a small drainage ditch to get to a wire fence. I went to work with a pair of pliers and the hacksaw blade. I manage to cut off some suitable lengths from the lower run of the horizontal wires, by so doing hoping that the fence would not be too drastically weakened and would still keep any livestock from escaping. Once I had some strands of wire, I had to re-cross the ditch, clamber back up the bank, to the road to arrive back at the car. The splint had been a desperate idea, but when needs must, the devil drives!

We selected a piece of wood for the splint, that was reasonably strong and yet was of the right size to fit as snugly as possible within the confines of the brace's angle. I proceeded to bind the wooden splint to the brace with the wire I had snipped from the fence. By carefully twisting the ends of the wire with the pliers I achieved a very tight binding. The trick worked and believe it or not, this temporary make-do-and-mend splint got us back home to Kent. Had it not looked obvious to anyone inspecting the car, our makeshift repair probably would have lasted out its life time; who knows. I was able to obtain and refit a replacement part later, once we were back in the UK. In the state it was, Droopy would certainly not have passed its MOT, had there been such a thing at that time.

Many of the roads in France are lined with trees. After our stop to mend the brace we saw many crashes, some serious, where vehicles had hit these trees. One lorry with a long bonnet was virtually split down the middle from the front to the back of the driver's cab. One way to demonstrate that it was strikingly obvious, that it was vitally important not to have defective steering on these tree-lined roads.

The truck is left-hand drive too!

We just had to be extra careful.

We got as far as Ardre, a few kilometres away from Calais and as we had two more days to spare, before our scheduled return on the Cross Channel ferry to Dover, we decided to branch off and head for Wissant, a short way down the coast near Boulogne. Wissant turned out to be a very pleasant place, where we relaxed until it was time for us to leave. The campsite was fine and just by a nice sandy beach, so we could take a dip in the sea, whenever the fancy took us. We made friends with a lively French girl called Claudine and a lovely Norwegian family.

Finally we took the coast road and over the hills back to the ferry at Calais. The hills were still peppered with bomb and shell craters, a stark reminder of the Second World War. The craters stood out white against the green of the grass, as the hills were formed of chalk just like the white Cliffs of Dover. They reminded me of a grotesque devil's golf course. I have visited this area since that time and it appears, that the craters have been filled in and any unexploded shells removed. Over time green vegetation has healed those scars naturally.

The rest of the journey from Wissant to Calais harbour and the Channel crossing was accomplished without further incident. We arrived home safely. It had not been so much a holiday as an adventure and it had certainly been an experience, which I for one, would never forget.

One could conclude from this tale, that we were somewhat foolhardy to have gone on such a trip so ill-prepared. It was only extreme good fortune and our guardian angels, that allowed us to reach home again at all, in one piece and let alone safely.

I never knew before that adventure that Guardian Angels could appear as if from   nowhere, just at the opportune moment, riding on motor scooters. Well they certainly did for us.

"Heart-Break?"

FINALE

I had to decide what to do about Droopy Drawers, my little car that had taken us on an adventurous tour and had given us so many frights. Not that we hadn't enjoyed the trip, but I had to face the facts: we were extremely fortunate to have been able to make it back home again. We had had more than our share of anxious moments and amazing luck in achieving repairs.

Whilst trying to come to a decision as to where I went from there, I did consider the possibility of fitting a new hydraulic braking system; conversion-kits were available on the market at the time. However, brakes were only one of her many problems. I decided that I wanted to be able to travel about in a vehicle that was watertight. I wanted something with more luggage space and more importantly, I wanted something that was reliable. It was all very well, but I decided that Droopy, attractive as she was, despite her charm, just had to go. I had to face up to the situation and to bite the bullet. In many ways it was a sad day, but I went ahead and advertised her for sale in the "Exchange and Mart" (a commercial sales outlet newspaper). My next worry was: could I sell her? Would anybody want to buy her, especially if I were to do the decent thing and came clean and point out all her failings to a would-be purchaser. My advertisement attracted one response. A smartly turned out man of about thirty to forty years old came round one evening by appointment. He had arrived by a combination of train and then taxi. He only had to cast his eyes on Dreamy Droopy, and it was a case of love at first sight. He was immediately smitten – just as I had been. I did make a point of informing him about all the repairs I had carried out and warned him, that the brakes needed attention. I offered him the chance to take Droopy out for a test drive, but he declined. He eagerly handed over his £60 (the asking price) in cash; which as the reader might remember, was precisely the price I had paid when I bought her. I wonder now, if I had been made aware of all Droopy's vices, as (to be fair) he was, then would I have still gone ahead with the purchase? Probably! Sucker!

I had quickly become a little bit more 'worldly-wise'.

On completion of the sale, and with the cash handed over, I was careful to write out a receipt or a sales document. Which, to make it look more official, I had put together with the aid of my father's typewriter. Included on it I wrote the following; '*as seen and inspected by.......................*' with spaces provided for him to write his name and address, and for him to sign and date it.

Signed ……………………… Date………………..….

The rather austere "Ragged Knickered Nora" (RKN) A ford 5 cwt* van that replaced Droopy.

Not perhaps presenting the usual image one would expect of a young man's dream machine.

It had fierce (rod operated) brakes, rock hard suspension, poor road holding and dreadfully restricted side and rear vision. It had an old bus seat in the front, and nothing in the back, but then when one thinks about it, Droopy only had two seats. Because it was a van, it was not subject to purchase tax. Strictly speaking it was limited to 30mph.

But Ragged Knickered Nora is another story.

*Hundred lbs (avoir du pois) weight.

Our map

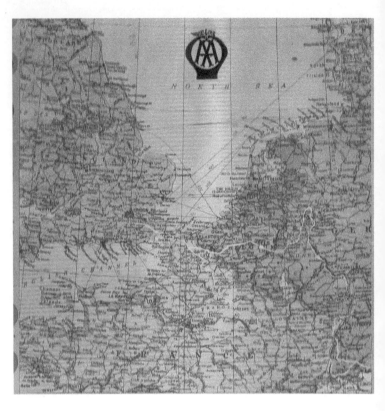

Our one and only map, which was supplied by the "A-A"
Our route is marked up in white.

Lightning Source UK Ltd.
Milton Keynes UK
UKHW012129130820
368207UK00002B/514